A Guide to...
Gouldian Finches
AND THEIR MUTATIONS
Revised Edition

Edited and Published by ABK Publications ©

Contributing Authors
Dr Rob Marshall BVSc MACVSc (Avian Health)
Dr Milton Lewis BSc (Hons) PhD
Ron Tristram
Dr Terry Martin BVSc

© ABK Publications 2005

First Published 1991 by
ABK Publications
PO Box 6288,
South Tweed Heads,
NSW 2486, Australia.

ISBN 0 9750817 1 3 soft cover
ISBN 0 9750817 2 1 hard cover

All rights reserved. No part of this publication may be reproduced, stored in any retrieval system, or transmitted in any form or by any means without the prior permission in writing of the publisher.

Disclaimer: Very few drugs are registered for use in birds, and most usages and dose rates have been extrapolated from mammalian therapeutics. Everyone using medications should be aware that manufacturers of these drugs will not accept any responsibility for the 'off-label' use of their drugs. The dose rates and information are based on clinical trials and practical experience, but unrecorded adverse side effects may occur. Where possible, the author has provided brand names for the drugs mentioned. These should not be taken as a recommendation for one particular brand over another, but rather as a starting point for you to find the drug of your choice. In most instances, contraindications and side effects are not listed. This should not be taken to mean that there are none—many of these drugs have not been used extensively, and reports on contraindications and side effects are not recorded at date of publication.

Front Cover:
Top left: Black-headed Normal cock — Peter Odekerken
Top right: Black-headed White-breasted Single Factor Pastel Blue cock — Peter Odekerken
Middle left: Red-headed Australian Yellow cock — James Watson
Centre: Red-headed White-breasted Dilute-backed hen — James Watson
Bottom centre: Red-headed Blue cock — Pieter van den Hooven
Bottom left: Yellow-headed Normal hen — Pieter van den Hooven
Bottom right: Red-headed Normal cock — Peter Odekerken

Back Cover:
Yellowtip Bill Black-headed Lutino hen — Cindy Godwin

Design, Type and Art: The TAG Studio
Printing: Kingswood Press

CONTENTS

CONTRIBUTING AUTHORS	7
ACKNOWLEDGEMENTS	9
INTRODUCTION	9

THE GOULDIAN FINCH IN THE WILD 10

Introduction	11
Taxonomy	11
Status	12
Population Monitoring	13
Distribution	14
Field Description of the Wild Gouldian Finch	15
Tropical Summer—Wet Season, Summer Food,	
Tropical Winter—Dry Season, Breeding in the Wild, Moult	
The Future of the Wild Gouldian Finch	23

THE GOULDIAN FINCH IN CAPTIVITY 25

HOUSING	26
Colony Housing	26
Susceptibility to the Effects of Cold and Wet Conditions	27
Housing in Temperate Regions	28
Housing in Tropical Regions	28
Indoor Housing in Cooler Regions	29
Housing Structures	29
Conventional Aviaries, Suspended Cages and Aviaries,	
Cabinet and Cage Breeding, Holding Cages	
Building Materials	32
Substrate	32
Nesting Receptacles	33
Feed Stations	34
Water	
Perches	35
Temperature and Humidity Control	35
Human Disturbance	36
Transportation	36
Carry Boxes	37
Quarantine	37
NUTRITION	38
Introduction	38
Protein	39
Minerals	39
Grit	
Vitamins	40
Carbohydrates	40
Fats	41
Nutritional Supplements	41
Dietary Cycles	41
Moult Diet	41

Non-breeding Diet	42
Pre-breeding Diet	42
Breeding Diet	43
Softfoods, Soaked and Sprouted Seeds	43
Softfoods, Soaked and Sprouted Seed—Soaked Seed Process, Sprouted Seed Process	
Dry Seed	46
Purchasing Seed, Seed Storage	
Water	47
BREEDING	47
Introduction	47
Selecting Stock	48
Establishing Breeding Pairs	49
Line Breeding	50
Incompatibility	52
Courtship Behaviour	52
Nest Preparation	53
Egg Laying and Incubation	54
Nestlings	54
Nestlings on the Floor	
Fledglings	55
Moult	55
Foster-parenting	56
Bengalese Finches as Foster-parents, Gouldian Finches as Foster-parents, Fostering Method	
Record Keeping	59
Breeding Mutations—Considerations	59
Health Difficulties in Mutations	61
MUTATIONS AND COLOUR BREEDING	62
Breeding Head Colours	63
Mating Expectations	63
TABLE OF MATING EXPECTATIONS	64
MUTATIONS	68
Blue	68
Seagreen	68
Sex-linked Pastel (Yellow-backed)	68
Dilute-backed	71
Australian Yellow	71
White-breasted	72
Lilac-breasted	72
Weak Mutations	73
RECESSIVE INHERITANCE TABLE	73
COLOUR MUTATIONS, GENETIC INHERITANCE & GENE ACTION	74
Which Head Colour is Wildtype?	74
PIGMENTATION AND COLOUR PRODUCTION	75
Head	77

Neck	77
Back and Wings	78
Rump and Tail	78
Breast	78
Belly	78
MUTATIONS	79
HEAD COLOURS	79
Black-headed	79
Yellow-headed	80
BODY COLOUR	82
Blue	82
Seagreen	83
Sex-linked Pastel (Yellow-backed)	84
Dilute-backed	89
Yellow (Australian Yellow)	91
White-breasted	93
Lilac-breasted	96
RARE MUTATIONS	97
Blue-breasted	97
Cinnamon	98
Japanese 'Red-eye Factor' (Fallow)	98
Lutino	99
Dark Factor	101
'Lime'	102
Turquoise ('Australian Blue')	103
'Dilute'	104
'Grey Factor'	104
'White-wing'	104
COLOUR COMBINATIONS	105
White-breasted Combinations	109
Halfsiders	116
Melanism	117
GLOSSARY OF TERMS	118

HEALTH AND DISEASE 120

Introduction	121
Health and Happiness in the Gouldian Finch	121
Essentials of Gouldian happiness	
Natural Behaviour and Health	122
General Susceptibility to Disease	122
Critical Periods for Gouldian Health	123
Nestlings, Juveniles, Breeding Birds, Identifying Weak Individuals	
DISEASE PREVENTION	124
Control of Mites and Lice	124
Worming	125
Coccidiosis Protection	125
Disease Prevention for Juvenile Gouldians	125

DIAGNOSIS OF DISEASES ... 126
Dropping Analysis ... 126
Antibiotics ... 127
Emergency First Aid ... 127
Earliest Symptoms of Illness ... 128
Tired Eyes (Lazy Eyelids), Inactivity, Change in Feather Colour, Fluffed-up Appearance, Droppings, Heavy Breathing, Hunched Appearance, Symptoms of Cold Stress, Noisy Respiration
Symptomatic Conditions and Treatments ... 129
Droppings ... 129
Size, Colour, Dirty Vent, Smell, Diarrhoea, Undigested Seed in Droppings
Feather Loss ... 131
On the Head, Around the Eye, Wing or Tail Feathers
Feet Problems ... 131
Beak Abnormalities ... 132
Beak Scratching ... 132
Eye Symptoms ... 132
Breathing Difficulties ... 132
Coughing or Sneezing, Respiratory Symptoms and Deaths, Respiratory Symptoms Associated with Vomiting, Respiratory Symptoms Failing to Respond to Antibiotic Treatment
Going Light ... 133
Vomiting ... 133
Head Twirling and Stargazing ... 133
Breeding Symptoms ... 133
Dead-in-Shell and Infertility, Stunted and Dying Nestlings, Sick and Dying Juveniles

DISEASES AND DISORDERS ... 135
Aspergillosis ... 135
Moulding Disease (Aflatoxicosis) ... 135
Campylobacter Infection ... 136
Coccidiosis ... 137
E. coli Infection ... 137
Megabacteria Infection (Avian Gastric Yeast) ... 138
Mite and Lice Infestations ... 139
Blood-sucking Mites, Epidermoptic Mites, Air Sac Mites
Ornithosis (*Chlamydophila*) Infection ... 140
Polyomavirus ... 142
Salmonella Infection ... 143
Streptococcal Infection ... 144
Thrush (*Candidiasis*) ... 145
Cochlosoma ... 146
Worms ... 147
Tapeworm (Cestodes)
Yersinia Infection ... 148

BIBLIOGRAPHY ... 149

CONTRIBUTING AUTHORS

DR ROB MARSHALL
BVSc MACVSc (Avian Health)

Rob Marshall has been keeping birds since 1960, beginning with pigeons. In 1975 he graduated with a degree in Veterinary Science and four years later established his existing practice, Carlingford Animal Hospital in Sydney, Australia. Rob continued his bird health studies in Germany, Holland and the USA. In 1988 he was awarded the MACVSc (Avian Health).

Rob's presentations, lectures and contributions to numerous magazines internationally are prolific. He has contributed to the health and disease sections of a number of the **'A Guide to...'** series titles published by **ABK Publications** and has written articles for **Australian BirdKeeper Magazine**, as well as writing his own books, including *Gouldian and Finch Health*.

In his practice, Rob has dealt with all species of pet birds and through his ongoing research has developed a range of nutritional supplements for pet and aviary birds.

In 1995 he was the veterinary consultant for the Northern Territory Nature and Conservation Commission for a scientific study of the disease status in wild populations of the endangered Gouldian Finch as it related to a 'Recovery Plan'. This entailed fieldwork on the endangered Gouldian Finch in the Kimberleys in Western Australia and in the Keep River National Park in the Northern Territory, funded by the Nature and Conservation Commission of the Northern Territory.

Rob contributed to the *Nutrition* chapter and prepared the *Health and Disease* chapters.

DR MILTON LEWIS BSc (Hons) PhD

Milton Lewis has had a long association with the Gouldian Finch both in aviculture and in his pursuits as a research scientist. At an early age while living in Canberra, Australia, Milton kept Gouldians under trying conditions with a minimum of information from other enthusiasts. He became resolved to understand as much as possible about this beautiful bird and eventually become successful in keeping and breeding this finch.

After completing an honours degree in Zoology at the Australian National University he accepted a PhD scholarship and a position as associate lecturer at James Cook University in North Queensland. This was a wonderful chance to both increase his scientific knowledge and research skills while at the same time moving to a climate where he could keep Gouldian Finches with relative ease.

While completing his investigation of the ecology and mating system of the Golden-headed Cisticola, a small Australian warbler, he undertook investigations of mate choice in Gouldian Finches with the assistance of his honours student Samantha Fox. Following this successful investigation of the role of face colour in mate selection he was rewarded with the opportunity to apply his extensive research skills to investigating the ecology of wild Gouldians in the Northern Territory. The groundwork for this project had been laid by his good friend and teacher Dr Sonia Tidemann but the answer as to why Gouldians were still rapidly disappearing in the wild remained speculative. Milton accepted the challenge and set forth to better understand the ecology of Gouldians under the difficult field conditions of tropical wet seasons in areas that other research scientists had been unable to thoroughly explore. It did not take long for him to realise that there were problems with seed availability and that this was probably related to the intensity of annual burning that takes place in that region of northern Australia. Unfortunately Milton was forced to return south before this research was complete but his love and endeavours to explore the ecology of this finch remain strong.

He continues to investigate the role of plumage colour patterns in mate choice in the Gouldian—Australia's most beautiful and popular finch—using captive populations. He hopes to again be able to continue his research on wild populations of this finch when the opportunity arises.

Milton's contributions to the chapters, *The Gouldian Finch in the Wild* and *The Gouldian Finch in Captivity*, were based on his academic research of both wild and captive birds and hands-on avicultural experiences.

RON TRISTRAM

Ron Tristram's first avian encounter, at nine years of age, comprised a pair of Budgerigars, one blue and one green, which were jointly owned with his sister. Two years later his father built him an aviary to keep canaries. These were followed by bullfinches, Zebra and Red-headed Finches. Subsequent to keeping finches for about six years, Ron built his first aviary to house a flock of more than 40 racing pigeons. A job transfer to Tweed Heads in Northern New South Wales in 1966 saw him replace aviculture with aquaculture. Later, after moving to Sydney and eventually purchasing his first house, Ron built a shed approximately 3.5 metres long x 2 metres wide to maintain his aquaculture activities. This was later converted to a breeding room for Budgerigars. His collection soon grew to include Peachfaced Lovebirds, Gouldian and other species of finches. Eleven years of breeding and showing Budgerigars followed—providing invaluable experience in colour breeding. In 1988/89 he made the decision to keep only Gouldian Finches. His entire aviary complex was rebuilt in 2001 to specifically house Gouldian Finches and provide a user-friendly environment for this exceptional Australian grassfinch.

Ron contributed to various chapters with his personal avicultural knowledge of the management and breeding of the Gouldian Finch in captivity.

DR TERRY MARTIN BVSc

Terry Martin was given his first pair of Zebra Finches at 10 years of age. He worked on the different colour mutations in this species, establishing a firm interest and basic knowledge of genetics. In 1988 Terry graduated with a degree in Veterinary Science from the University of Queensland.

Terry has dedicated his ongoing studies on birds to the area of genetics and colour mutations and is highly respected in his research field internationally.

He has presented at avian and veterinary meetings and conferences, contributed articles to various publications including **Australian BirdKeeper Magazine** and various **ABK Publication** titles and authored the book **A Guide to Colour Mutations and Genetics in Parrots** published by **ABK Publications**.

In 1999 Terry initiated the formation of an international genetics discussion group on parrot species. Writing the parrot genetics book became an even greater stimulus for knowledge and has led to further contact with researchers in parrot and more general avian genetics worldwide.

Terry's interest in avian genetics covers all avicultural species and he participates in multiple discussion groups covering the genetics of Gouldian Finches, Zebra Finches and Colourbred Canaries as well as parrots. For this book, he has updated the original chapters on *Mutations and Colour Breeding* and has contributed extensive new work dealing with Gouldian Finch mutations from a more technical viewpoint. He also assisted in the sourcing and selection of mutation photographs throughout this book.

ACKNOWLEDGEMENTS

The publisher and contributing authors would like to thank the following people for their support and assistance in the preparation of this revised book—Dr Danny Brown BVSc (Hons) BSc (Hons) MACVSc (Avian Health) and Dr Stacey Gelis BVSc (Hons) MACVSc (Avian Health). We also acknowledge and thank the following people for their photographic assistance—Dr Danny Brown BVSc (Hons) BSc (Hons) MACVSc (Avian Health), Dr Michael Cannon BVSc MACVSc (Avian Health), Don Crawford, Mike Fidler, Herschell Fry, Cindy Godwin, Ian Hinze, Russell Kingston, Ray and Wendy Lowe, Winnie McAlpin, Laraine McGinnis, Joanne McGinnis, Yoshihiro Miyake, Anthony Mobbs, David Myers, Peter Odekerken, Eric Otway, Glenn Roman, John Sammut, Kevin Solomon, Michael Tristram, Dirk van den Abeele, Pieter van den Hooven, James Watson and Greg Wightman.

Dr Milton Lewis would like to thank his family—parents, grandparents, wife Carol and children Andrea and Ashly for their ongoing support of his research projects and other endeavours. He also acknowledges the guidance and support of colleagues and mentors, David Lawson, Chris Johnson and Andrew Cockburn, Steve Pruett-Jones, David Hooper, John McKean and fellow volunteer Gouldian Finch watchers Kevin Solomon and Ted and Kerry Davenport. Finally, he would like to thank the Gouldian Finch, especially individuals like *yb-NM*. Without them his knowledge of this species would be very limited indeed.

Ron Tristram wishes to thank Glen Bowden for his continued support and his son Michael for all his photographic work for this book.

Dr Terry Martin would like to thank Daniel Wildermeersch of Belgium, who introduced him to a number of breeders of rare Gouldian Finch mutations from around the world. Daniel is owner of the web site Erythrura, possibly the best site about Gouldian Finches and parrotfinches on the internet and located at http://users.skynet.be/fa398872/navfram.en.htm

INTRODUCTION

The first edition of this extremely popular title, co-authored by John Sammut and Dr Rob Marshall and published in 1991, set a valuable and informative base for this revision.

Over time various ideas and methods of managing and breeding Gouldian Finches have evolved, including research in nutritional, health and genetic aspects.

For this revision we have consulted with Ron Tristram, Dr Milton Lewis BSc (Hons) PhD, Dr Rob Marshall BVSc, MACVSc (Avian Health) and Dr Terry Martin BVSc. Drawing from their various areas of experience and expertise we have produced this title with the most up-to-date and valuable information on Gouldian Finches.

It must be noted that there is information in this book which may not necessarily be the opinion of all contributing authors. In particular, Ron Tristram, who has been of enormous assistance to the production of this revision, wishes to distance himself from any reference to or support of the practice of using Bengalese Finches to foster Gouldian Finches, which he believes is ultimately detrimental to the species.

ABK Publications has edited the material in such a way as to provide the reader with an array of relevant information which you can assimilate and utilise accordingly.

We sincerely hope that you gain in your experience and success with the breeding of this special species.

ABK Publications

THE GOULDIAN FINCH IN THE WILD

Red-headed Normal Gouldian Finch cock

P ODEKERKEN

Introduction

Our understanding of the ecology of the wild Gouldian Finch *Erythrura gouldiae*, which is endemic to Australia, is surprisingly contradictory. Scientifically and aviculturally we know a great deal, yet over time some of this knowledge has become distorted. One account that comes to mind is the reference to the Gouldian Finch's *migratory* behaviour (Strahan 1996). This appears to be misinterpreted with the movements of Gouldian Finches being better described as short (less than 50km), irregular but seasonal, perhaps even nomadic in some instances, as was suggested originally by Immelmann (1977). There are numerous questions to be answered and the following sections endeavour to provide the reader with field observations and data collected over many years. This information often remains in observers' notebooks or other inaccessible places, never becoming available to those people who might value it most—the keepers of the Gouldian Finch. It is hoped that this knowledge and understanding of wild Gouldian Finches will benefit everyone in their attempts to keep this species successfully.

For many people seeing a Gouldian Finch in the wild is just a dream. Those enthusiasts who do see these fantastic birds usually do so early in the morning at a quiet secluded waterhole and the experience becomes somewhat religious. It was possibly the same for early naturalists when they first came across what should be described as the jewel of Australian birds. John Gould recognised the beauty of this finch when he named it in honour of his late wife Elizabeth for her dedication in illustrating wildlife and accompanying him to Australia on field excursions (Gould in Strahan 1996).

A magnificent wild Red-headed Gouldian Finch cock peering into the water before taking a drink. Note the sheen of the feathers and the extent of the blue behind the mask and on the wing coverts.

Gouldian Finches were collected during the early explorations of northern Australia and taken back to Europe for both private collections and museums.

Taxonomy

The Gouldian Finch is an Estrildid carrying a variety of morphological features that have caused confusion about its relationships and ancestry with other finches. Previously the Gouldian Finch has been considered a grassfinch, genus *Poephila*, because of the bill and wing shape as well as the finely attenuated central tail pins (Delacour 1943; Morris 1958). Hall (1962) considered Gouldian Finches to be closely allied to the genus *Lonchura* (the Asian mannikin group) because of colour pattern and song. Although many texts still refer to the Gouldian Finch as belonging to a monotypic genus *Chloebia* (Ziswiler *et al* 1972; Goodwin 1982; Clement *et al* 1993), on the basis of recent evidence it is now widely accepted that this species belongs with the parrotfinch genus *Erythrura* (Christidis and Boles 1994).

In terms of similarities the taxonomic position of the Gouldian Finch as one of the

Nestling Gouldian Finches displaying the characteristic blue bill nodules that are found on all 'parrotfinches'.

parrotfinches is sensible. Gouldian Finches exhibit the vivid green back colour, the facial mask and most importantly the blue luminous beak tubercles (nodules) of the nestlings. In addition, and often not mentioned in other texts, many of the parrotfinch species also possess elongated central tail feathers of varying lengths.

On the other hand Gouldian Finches have been rejected as being parrotfinches because they lacked the red rump that appears to be characteristic of the group. However this is probably a secondarily derived change of colour as are many of the other unique colours of the Gouldian Finch. This change in colour may have occurred in conjunction with the Gouldian Finch's change of habitat to open grassland, leaving behind the closed forest and forest edges of its nearest relatives.

As a parrotfinch, the Gouldian Finch is one of 12 species within a genus that is distributed within the Indo-Malayan region, the Philippines, New Guinea, New Caledonia, Samoa, Fiji and northern Australia (Goodwin 1982). Unfortunately five of these species are now listed as threatened and in need of protection. They are the Gouldian Finch *Erythrura gouldiae* (Endangered C2b), the Red-eared Parrotfinch *E. coloria* (Lower Risk/Near Threatened), the Pink-billed Parrotfinch *E. kleinschmidti* (Endangered C2b), the Royal Parrotfinch *E. regia* (Vulnerable C2a) and the Green-faced Parrotfinch *E. viridifacies* (Vulnerable A1cd & 2cd).

Status

The most frequently asked question about Gouldian Finches in the wild is, 'Are they really endangered?' The wild Gouldian Finch is a particularly challenging species to find and observe because of its propensity to live in rugged, inaccessible country. This habit has severely limited our ability to answer basic ecological questions reliably. Gouldian Finches have been listed as endangered by Garnett *et al* (2000) on the basis of guidelines developed by international authorities for recognising species in trouble. The status of the Gouldian Finch was maintained as endangered when last reviewed by Dostine (1998). This decision was made because it was thought that there were fewer than 250 adult individuals within any population, that there were fewer than 10 populations remaining

Typical woodland savanna near the Drysdale River in Western Australia where wild Gouldian Finches are frequently encountered.

within the wild, and that the species had suffered a serious decline in population size. Based on knowledge at the time of review this was the best decision. However, after further research, it is increasingly difficult to justify this species as nationally endangered. There are now more than 10 documented sites within the wild in both the Northern Territory and Western Australia where the populations are likely to exceed 250 adults. This does not even take into account the numerous smaller populations that also remain within the Northern Territory and Western Australia. In Queensland, however, the species is poorly represented by wild populations at a state level and should still be considered as endangered (Garnett pers. comm.).

Small waterholes, often dotted throughout the landscape of northern Australia, are visited daily by Gouldian and other finches.

Population Monitoring

Assessing the status of any species is complicated and always comes back to the basics of how many birds remain in the wild. Although many accounts of Gouldian Finch numbers indicate that in the past the birds congregated in large flocks of hundreds of birds there is still some room for doubt (Franklin *et al* 1999). Former professional trappers like Ray Ackroyd have a depth of knowledge about this species that has perhaps not been given full acknowledgement. His account indicates that although Gouldians were easier to find 30 years ago the species was never truly common (pers. comm.). Gouldian Finches were highly valued by legal trappers. They fetched better prices than other finches, being fewer in number and difficult to catch. It may be that because of their beauty, their obviousness in a group of other finches and perhaps their value as a discussion piece, that the rarity of the Gouldian Finch has been exaggerated over time.

Population size, as a determinant of the species' endangered status, is difficult to apply because it is almost impossible to estimate accurately. Between 1999 and 2003 annual counts of adult Gouldian Finches in the Yinberrie Hills in the Northern Territory fluctuated around a core population of about 200–250 adults and slightly more juveniles. This is currently the largest population being studied in Australia. Of the populations of Gouldian Finches now counted using standardised methods none match the abundance of the Yinberrrie Hills (Lewis pers. observ.). This area was very well surveyed and these estimates should be the best currently available. More than 100 waterholes were mapped within an environment that most people would consider totally devoid of water. Long-term local knowledge should allow higher levels of precision and accuracy

Families of wild Gouldian Finches often come together when drinking and feeding.

in estimating the population numbers but with such knowledge came an awareness of the many shortfalls in the estimating process.

Estimates of the population size of the Gouldian Finch were made by counting the number of individuals drinking each morning at known waterholes within the few accessible areas. Sitting, armed with binoculars and mugs of coffee, numerous volunteers watched patiently and tallied the birds as they flew in to drink from the cold water as the sun rose across the hills. On some mornings there were minor difficulties—birds just about to drink were disturbed by a goshawk, and then not seen again at that waterhole for the rest of the morning. However, for the most

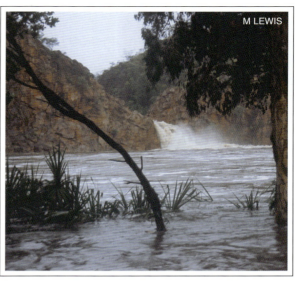

Creeks become raging torrents during the Wet Season.

part this process worked well and numerous people gained first-hand experience with the wild Gouldians.

Each year every effort was made to count the finches at all waterholes but it was always known that more waterholes existed within the hills than could easily be reached each morning. Annual estimates depended on the availability of water. In years after a heavy Wet Season there were numerous waterholes throughout the hills, in fact too many to count. In some cases, some waterholes were covered to try and force birds to use only monitored pools for drinking (Forrester and Wood 1999). In drier years there were fewer waterholes and covering them was not necessary. Intuitively you might think that fewer waterholes would be good with all the birds being forced to use just those remaining watering points. Unfortunately fewer waterholes recorded fewer birds. Had birds moved to areas that were not being counted or had birds perished as the water disappeared? At best, the counts were underestimates but the real purpose of the counts was not to produce data on whether there were 248 birds or 250 birds, but rather to monitor the gross fluctuations in population numbers. The priority was to try and understand why there were only 50 birds this year where there were 250 birds last year. To understand what had happened to cause the change in numbers would result in a better understanding of the ecology of the Gouldian Finch. The long-term plan was to sustain an increase in Gouldian Finch numbers in the wild.

Distribution

The past distribution of the Gouldian Finch is recognised as extending across all of tropical northern Australia (Slater *et al* 1986; Pizzey 1980; Pizzey 2003). This was possibly an exaggeration where previously the distribution of any species was determined by gathering all known sightings of birds, marking these sites on a map and shading the areas in between to form a distribution map. In the case of the Gouldian Finch with specific habitat requirements this method was grossly inaccurate. Most distribution records for the Gouldian Finch occur along main roads

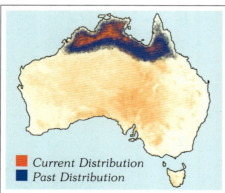

Distribution of Gouldian Finch.

Woodland savanna in the Bradshaw Station region of the Victoria River District, Northern Territory. Recent surveys indicated that Gouldian Finches were still plentiful at this site.

extending across north-western Australia from Katherine in the Northern Territory along the Gibb River Road to Broome in Western Australia. This is to be expected as the country to the north is mostly inaccessible to the majority of people because of the terrain and private land ownership.

The preferred habitat of the Gouldian Finch is savanna woodland with a native grass understorey and permanent water. This habitat has a patchy distribution across a belt of northern Australia that does not extend into desert regions and rarely makes contact with the coast. In the first instances where early naturalists and trappers collected the Gouldian Finch this range was greater and is shown by the presence of specimens from Darwin and Port Essington in the Northern Territory in the Tring Museum in the UK, along with accounts of flocks of Gouldians along the fringes of mangroves (Strahan 1996). Unfortunately the decline of the Gouldian Finch has forced the containment of remaining populations within small strongholds of relatively undisturbed habitat within the centre of the former more extensive range.

Gouldian Finches were well represented in early museum collections which contained a wide variety of ages as well as examples of each head colour.

Field Description of the Wild Gouldian Finch

The following account of Gouldian Finches in the wild has been gleaned mostly from a population within the Yinberrie Hills in the Northern Territory. This area had a long history of being valued by trappers as well as being a study site for research

A view of the Yinberrie Hills, Northern Territory.

scientists such as Dr Sonia Tidemann and the author (Milton Lewis). Sometimes it is difficult to take knowledge about a species gained at one site and apply it elsewhere. This is not the purpose of this chapter. Nor has it been written to assist future research scientists to find and understand the species. This work has been compiled to give an account of the annual activities of the Gouldian Finch in order to provide a better understanding of the requirements and preferences of the species in the wild as an aid to keeping them successfully in captivity.

Tropical Summer—Wet Season

In northern Australia only two seasons exist—wet and dry. The first heavy rain of the Wet Season in Katherine in the Northern Territory commences in December and often lasts until the end of February or early March.

Afternoon showers and storms provide the trigger for the flowering of numerous grasses and an escape from the build-up of the heat and humidity prior to the Wet Season.

This varies substantially from year to year with minor falls of rain often occurring in October and November. The humidity during this period can be above 80% and the temperature around 38°C. This climate is an integral component in the life cycle of the wild Gouldian Finch and controls daily and weekly activities.

Summer Food

With the rain comes the awakening of termites as countless millions of winged alates take to the air in search of mates and new places to start colonies. For most birds, including Hooded Parrots and other finches this is a feast. However, for the Gouldian Finch, little changes. Long-tailed Grassfinches and Hooded Parrots delight in gorging on mountains of nutritious insects while Gouldian Finches, only a few metres away, scrounge around for what appears to be old seed stuck between rocks on the ground. Close inspection reveals that they are eating germinating seed and we all know how beneficial sprouted seed is for getting our birds through the moult and into breeding condition. Unlike the Gouldian Finches described by Immelmann (1977), birds in the Yinberrie Hills have not been seen eating termites or other insects. Although these Gouldians may not be feeding on termites they are nevertheless enjoying a highly nutritious diet.

Sorghum begins to grow from seeds lying dormant on the ground early after the first rains of the Wet Season.

Clumps of Cockatoo Grass tend to occur in water-logged depressions in the lowlands around the breeding sites.

During about the second week of December Gouldians from the Yinberrie Hills can be found on the lower alluvial slopes between numerous watercourses that dissect an area termed the 'lowlands'. Gouldian Finches occupy these areas at this time of year because of better food resources. Rain falls in the lowlands before it does in the 'hills', producing the first flush of fresh seed in more than nine months. The seasonal pattern in the choice of seed is normally based upon availability. Cockatoo Grass *Alloteropsis semialata* is the first to ripen followed by Golden Beard Grass *Chrysopogon fallax* and then Soft Spinifex *Triodia bitextura*.

Cockatoo Grass grows along the edges of watercourses within heavier alluvial soil and is only taken by the birds where it occurs in thick clumps with a heavy seed-set. Seed production in this grass species is influenced to a great extent by fire and most seed appears after an early Dry Season fire followed by a season or two of rest. This seed is oval, slightly flattened and positioned in rows usually along three panicles (tufts), with a shape resembling commercial canary seed.

The next seed of the season is Golden Beard Grass, locally referred to as spear grass. This grows in drier soil about halfway up the sides of hills. The seeds of this species are large and hang like pendulums from tall stems. Because both Cockatoo Grass and Golden Beard Grass are also the preferred food of feral animals such as pigs and horses there has now been a need to

The large stems of Cockatoo Grass provide ample seed of similar appearance to commercial canary seed during a period of the year when fresh seed is just becoming available.

Cockatoo Grass provides highly palatable seeds for Gouldian Finches during the first weeks of the Wet Season.

Golden Beard Grass grows in thick patches on the sides of the hills throughout the lowland Wet Season feeding areas.

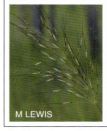

Golden Beard Grass is one of the important sources of seed for Gouldian Finches in the early Wet Season.

This early Wet Season burn exposes new supplies of seed for finches and releases trapped nitrogen for new growth of grass.

The growth of Cane Grass is also influenced by fire, but in this case it appears that small fires every few years actually increase the amount of seed produced, unlike many of the other grasses.

Hundreds of tiny spinifex seeds sit packed between glumes, late in the Wet Season before the Gouldian Finches leave to breed in the hills.

Spear Grass covers much of the Yinberrie Hills and has evolved to cope with hot Dry Season fires.

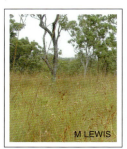

Kangaroo Grass occurs in large patches along creeks in the Yinberrie Hills.

It can take years for spinifex plants to recover from fire before again providing seed for finches.

Some spear grasses like Cane Grass grow around the hills of breeding sites and develop huge seeds packed with carbohydrate. These seeds provide breeding birds with much needed energy to carry out daily activities during the breeding season.

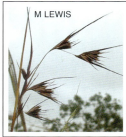

Kangaroo Grass is occasionally taken as food by Gouldian Finches late in the Wet Season or early in the Dry Season.

In good years, where fire has not occurred in the grasslands for long periods, spinifex provides ample seed that is essential for a successful breeding season.

place protective fencing around important Gouldian Finch feeding sites to exclude these competitive pests. Fire also influences seed production in this grass. Again, consistent annual hot burning produces poor crop yields but lack of burning also reduces seed yield significantly. Moderation is the answer with cooler, Wet Season or early Dry Season fires every three or more years, occasionally punctuated by a hotter fire perhaps every 10 years.

In some years, possibly the best years for Gouldian Finch survival, birds can be seen feeding on the tiny seeds of Soft Spinifex. In the Yinberrie Hills this grass occurs in very small tussocks mostly along the ridges of hills in well-drained, granitic soils. When this grass produces seed it does so profusely with around 800 or more seeds per stem and sometimes as many as 30 stems per plant. Gouldians relish this seed and grasp bunches of stems, feeding within the same clump of plants for hours, before moving on to find more food. Very few people have ever observed this activity (Dostine et al 2002; Lewis pers. observ.). Without fire this plant apparently takes several years to flower and produce an abundance of seed. In patches of spinifex studied more recently, those plants burnt in the previous year do not even produce flowers and in the second year flowers are produced in low numbers without fertile seed (Lewis 2003; Lewis in review). Most interesting and

Savanna grasses are tall and thick at the end of the Wet Season and laden with abundant seed.

Courtship displays by Gouldian Finch cocks occur most often late in the Wet Season.

Salmon Gum provides the best nesting sites for Gouldian Finches within the Yinberrie Hills in the Northern Territory.

perhaps the key to future management is the realisation that successful reproduction in Gouldian Finches more than doubles during the season after birds feed on these abundant supplies of spinifex seed. An opportunity now exists for land managers in these areas to put into action steps such as limiting hot Dry Season fires in the savanna grasslands to promote high seed production of spinifex and other native grasses.

After the flushes of seed have disappeared from the grasses of the lowlands there appears to be little reason for the Gouldians to stay in these areas. They then make the short move back up into the hills. At this time the seeds of the Giant Spear Grass *Heteropogon triticeus* are available in ample supplies, along with the first seeds of Spear Grass *Sorghum intrans* and Kangaroo Grass *Themeda triandra*. These are all large seeds and during this time of year are taken fresh from the stem just before they are completely ripe.

Wild Black-headed Gouldian Finch hen in breeding condition. Note her characteristic black bill.

In February or March Gouldian Finches look and feel their best, and begin selecting mates and nesting sites. Cocks sing actively and can be heard uttering the soft zitting trills used in courtship. In fact they become so receptive to these calls that even poor copies produced by human observers will bring cocks down from the treetops to investigate the sound. Significant time is devoted to inspecting nesting hollows, and cocks are often seen going in and out of hollow tree spouts, occasionally joined by a hen for a closer inspection. Gouldian Finch hens also show the signs of imminent nesting activity as their bills begin to change from glossy white to charcoal. Birds and humans can still enjoy the cooling effect of an afternoon shower and there is both ample water and feed. This is a good time for the Gouldian Finch in the Yinberrie Hills.

Tropical Winter—Dry Season

The change of the seasons can be quick and dramatic in northern Australia. The air lacks the heavy feel of moisture, the skies clear and the nights cool a little to somewhat more respectable temperatures (18–23°C). The month of April in the Yinberrie Hills carries the sound of fledgling Gouldians following their father around as he endeavours

Fresh growth of Cockatoo Grass denotes the boundary of an early Dry Season fire.

The seeds from these sorghum plants growing throughout the hills will provide much of the nourishment for Gouldian Finches throughout the Dry Season and during breeding.

to keep their appetites satiated. In the wild, the cocks appear to do most of the rearing of the fledglings while the hens regain their strength and start the next clutch. Grasses now begin to dry and the first of the season's fires appear within the landscape. The first fires are small, relatively low in intensity—and beneficial. Thick layers of dead grass and leaf litter cover seed that has fallen to the ground, making it difficult for finches to find (Woinarski 1990). Fires provide easier access to these patches of seed so it is important in the Yinberrie Hills at this time of the year that fires are used in moderation to make the Dry Season seed supplies readily available. Importantly, unlike the grasses found in the lowlands, Spear Grass has evolved seeds that are resistant to fire and are still full of nutrients after burning. This very 'oily' seed is probably a very important component of the diet for survival through colder nights. This species of grass appears to be the staple seed for most of the Dry Season (Dostine et al 2002) but there are also other seeds taken, including Love Grass (Lewis pers. observ.).

It is normal to observe small flocks of Gouldians foraging together, often with several other species such as the Long-tailed Grassfinch or the Masked Finch. As seed at this time of the year is only found on the ground this is where flocks are found feeding (Lewis pers. observ.). At the beginning of the Dry Season most groups will be composed of pairs and their young but as the season progresses juveniles will form larger flocks and disperse away from the adults. Foraging occurs throughout the day but the most intense period is midmorning from about 8.00–10.00am. It is interesting to note that even with the vivid adult plumage of a Gouldian Finch cock they are difficult to see as they search for seed. With heads down and green backs exposed, birds melt into the landscape. Observers often approach to within a few metres before hearing the familiar calls and realise that a flock is close.

Apart from finding seed, the most important part of the daily routine for the Gouldian

Left: A very young wild Gouldian Finch feeling the cold of the early morning.
Right: Wild Black-headed Gouldian Finch cock drinking from a secluded waterhole early in the morning.

A group of adult and young Gouldian Finches waiting to go down to the waterhole early in the morning.

Finch is finding water. Within the northern landscape water becomes sparse and only occurs in isolated pools during the Dry Season. Drinking mostly occurs during the early morning but to some extent is scheduled around the previous night's temperature. After a cool night, birds may arrive a little later, perhaps at around 8.00–8.30am but if the night has been more pleasant birds will start arriving as early as 7.00am.

The first individuals to arrive—often adult cocks—will do so quietly, often going unnoticed by the inexperienced waterhole observer. However, as the morning proceeds, small groups of both adults and juveniles will begin to arrive and perch in large trees adjacent to the waterholes, within observing distance of activity around the water's edge. Flocks can be seen circling several times in the sky around the general area before settling in the trees. These birds sit for as long as half an hour in the full sun. Perhaps they are warming their cold, small bodies, or perhaps they are searching the area for predators such as the Australian Goshawk *Accipiter fasciatus*, that take unsuspecting finches as food. On occasions when predators are at the waterholes the flocks of Gouldian Finches will fly away, probably to a safer waterhole. If the area is safe, birds will start to fly down to perch in another smaller tree closer to the water and then finally come down to drink. Drinking takes only a few seconds and the birds then disappear from the area. As with other Estrildid finches, Gouldian Finches drink by sucking (Zann 1996) and are able to take enough water quickly to satisfy their daily intake. During the incubation period it is rare to observe Gouldian Finch adults drinking more than once a day, although some individuals do visit waterholes again late in the afternoon (Lewis pers. observ.).

The most favoured waterholes are quite small, perhaps a metre in length, half a metre wide and very shallow (5–10cm). Pools are often located in rock outcrops and may have a small sandy beach along one side where the birds approach the water's edge. Gouldian Finches prefer clean water, undisturbed by animals such as cattle, horses and water buffalo. There are many accounts of birds drinking from water in depressions made by cattle hooves but it is likely that in these areas there are no other places to drink. During the early part of the Dry Season in the Kimberley region of Western Australia and in the Gulf of Carpentaria Gouldian Finches drink only from clear pools on rock outcrops. However, as the season progresses, they are forced to frequent pools where cattle are also drinking the last remaining water (Lewis pers. observ.). Gouldian Finches will also visit cattle troughs which provide abundant fresh clean water (Ackroyd pers. comm.; Lewis pers. observ.). When visiting a cattle trough birds prefer to drink from either the

Eucalypts often referred to as 'Snappy Gums' are preferred nest trees for Gouldian Finches throughout northern Australia.

overflow or the drips from the outflow pipe or overflow rather than out of the trough.

Breeding continues during the Dry Season depending on water and seed availability but in most years it is possible to observe fledglings still displaying their luminescent beak nodules well into August. It appears that in some respects the Gouldian Finch is opportunistic, breeding only when resources are available, although to a much lesser extent than species such as the Zebra Finch.

Unlike most other finches the Gouldian Finch only nests within tree hollows formed by termites, although there are reports of nests in termite mounds. The preferred species of trees are often referred to as 'snappy gum' because of the high incidence of these trees losing limbs during periods of wind before and after the Wet Season. In the Yinberrie Hills the Salmon Gum *Eucalyptus tintinnans* is the main supplier of nests but in other regions Snappy Gum *Eucalyptus brevifolia* provides hollows. Although these trees grow throughout the hills of northern Australia, Gouldian Finches are particular about the trees they select for hollows. In the Yinberrie Hills, they prefer Salmon Gums growing on rocky slopes without a dense understorey (Tidemann et al 1992a) and more specifically trees that occur with no other tree species (monotypic stands) that receive the first of the sun's warming rays in the morning (Lewis pers. observ.).

Breeding in the Wild

Cocks appear to do most of the nest building. In many instances nests are merely a bed of coarse grass, usually Spear Grass with a thin layer of finer stems from grasses such as White Grass *Sehima nervosum* and Love Grass (Lewis pers. observ.). Cocks and hens share the incubation but hens play the major role doing all the night sitting as well as a share of the day duties. A clutch of 3–5 eggs is normal and about 75% of clutches fledge young (Tidemann et al 1999). Eggs are laid daily during the early morning and hatch between 14 days (Tidemann et al 1999) and 17 days (Lewis pers. observ.) after incubation has commenced. Incubation appears to begin after the third egg in the clutch has been laid.

Spear Grass seed lying dormant during the Dry Season provides the bulk of the Gouldian Finch diet.

Although nesting success is good in comparison with other wild bird populations, only 15–16% of adults breed at each site (Tidemann et al 1999), reducing the potential reproductive output of the population. Both parents feed the young in the nest on a diet of Spear Grass and continue feeding until the young fledge at about 20–21 days of age. This has been determined by watching adults feed and by inspecting the crops of nestlings. However it is likely that other varieties of seed are also used but to a lesser extent. Because the seeds of *Schizachyrium* sp. are generally smaller and are pushed to the bottom of the crop underneath the larger Spear Grass seeds they go unnoticed during crop inspection. After fledging, the young are fed for several weeks and remain with the adults during this period. As the Dry Season progresses young Gouldian Finches leave the safety and care of the parents to join other juveniles, and occasionally other species of finches before roaming the hills in search of food.

Moult

The moult in wild Gouldian Finches commences slowly and can go almost unnoticed during the middle of August and early September (Tidemann et al 1994, Woinarski et al 1992). Prior to the moult the appearance of the adult plumage shows extreme amounts of wear—feathers are dull and the edges of the wing and tail are frayed. In adult hens the plumage of the belly and chest is particularly worn and discoloured with charcoal that has been rubbed from the ground during feeding. Juveniles are first to begin the moult with the sequential replacement of primaries, starting with the inner first feather until the last outer primary is lost. As the last of the primaries are being replaced, the body moult begins with the rump and tail-covert feathers. This is quickly followed by feathers on the belly, chest and back. The final body feathers to be renewed are on the forehead, throat and chin. In some juveniles the secondaries are only partially replaced or not replaced at all while the last of the body feathers are being renewed. The moult in juveniles is much slower than that of adults and is usually completed by the middle of December. Adult Gouldian Finches commence their moult a little later, in October, and most of the population have finished by late November. The sequence of feather loss in adults is the same as in juveniles. However adult Gouldian Finches replace all secondary wing feathers.

A young, wild Gouldian Finch cock partially through his first moult.

The moulting period is highly stressful for both adult and juvenile Gouldian Finches and it is during this period that the highest mortality is presumed to occur, particularly in juveniles. Individual birds continually lose weight as feathers are lost and replaced. In some instances as much as 20% of the total body weight is lost during the months of the moult and this is not replaced until the renewal of the feathers is complete (Lewis pers. observ.). In the wild the moulting period also coincides with highly stressful weather conditions and the months of lowest food availability in the year. The months of October and November are exceedingly hot, with temperatures above 38°C, high humidity and sometimes severe storms. Seed on the ground at this time of year is old, low in nutrients and difficult to extract from between the crevices in rocks. There is perhaps a little improvement in conditions when rain occurs and birds are able to feed on the germinating seed. However, if the time between rains is too long this causes another period without seed because all the fertile seed has germinated and grown past a point where it is useful to the birds. During this time birds are waiting until the first of the new seeds appear in December which could mean several weeks of very low quality food.

The Red-headed Gouldian Finch.

The Future of the Wild Gouldian Finch

The yearly cycle for the wild Gouldian has now been described in the briefest terms. It is pertinent to conclude with a short summary of reasons for the Gouldian Finch's demise in the wild and where ecological land management should be targeted in the future to allow this species to remain in the wild.

In the past there have been a variety of well-publicised, plausible scenarios that may have indirectly or directly resulted in fewer wild Gouldian Finches.

A striking, wild Black-headed Gouldian Finch cock making the most of the early morning sun.

The role of pastoral practices and land management in the reduction of Gouldian Finch numbers were investigated (Tidemann 1986). This was followed by research into how Air Sac Mite, the parasite *Sternostoma tracheacolum*, was involved in the Gouldian Finch decline (Tidemann et al 1992b). Diet analysis showed that Gouldian Finches are specialist seasonal foragers of native grass seeds (Dostine et al 2001; Dostine et al 2002).

Reproductively the Gouldian Finch is an enigma—being highly fecund yet still declining in the wild (Tidemann et al 1999). All of these investigations were touching on what is undoubtedly a very complex problem where a variety of factors are now impinging upon the health of wild Gouldians. Sonia Tidemann (pers. comm.) agrees that what we are now seeing in the wild is a species of bird that is immuno-compromised, allowing a variety of diseases and other factors to reduce the life spans of the birds.

In an aviary situation caring for birds is relatively easy because we are able to monitor individuals daily, remove sick birds and quickly administer measures to halt the loss of birds. We go to extraordinary lengths to ensure that birds have only the best quality seed and the purest water. This is not an easy task for an ecologist to accomplish working in a 100km² aviary where almost nothing can be controlled.

In the case of the Gouldian Finch, water appeared to be clean and readily available throughout the year even if the birds had to travel some distance each day to find the pools. Seed in the Dry Season also appeared to be abundant although limited in quality toward the end of the season. Seed in the Wet Season, however, appeared to be located in very small patches kilometres apart.

Researchers had difficulty locating birds during this period so there were few observations and little data regarding the behaviour of Gouldian Finches. In recent years it had been noticed that there was a correlation—in seasons with high breeding success the preceding Dry Season had suffered fewer fires in the lowland Wet Season feeding areas.

With this background information the relationship between fire and seed production in native grasses was explored with astonishing results. It was found that a complex relationship exists between fire and flora in northern Australia. Fires promote and reduce the amount of seed produced by native grasses and therefore impinge on the reproductive success of birds using that seed as a resource.

The Yinberrie Hills after a severe, late Dry Season fire.

There are a great number of new threats to the survival of the Gouldian Finch in northern Australia. Industries such as tourism are expanding, mining corporations continue to explore for new wealth and pastures are now being managed to improve livestock production with grasses unpalatable for our native fauna. Perhaps the bright light on the horizon is that there is now an understanding of how to better manage fires to produce more high quality seed for the Gouldian Finch. This will result in healthier populations that can better withstand the future pressures as modernisation pushes back the frontiers of northern Australia.

HOUSING

Gouldian Finches can be adequately housed in a variety of ways. The method you employ will depend on the aim of the breeding program. If you are attempting to provide environmental conditions similar to those experienced by Gouldian Finches in the wild then the use of aviary flights is more appropriate than small cabinets or cages. The general consensus is that birds flown in flights have ample space to exercise, which is essential for good health and successful breeding. In this form of housing the finches appear to produce better results than those housed in boxes or cabinets. This breeding strategy is being addressed at the Western Plains Zoo near Dubbo in New South Wales and at the Territory Wildlife Park in Darwin where wild Gouldian Finches are currently being managed for future release programs.

A fine example of a planted aviary owned by Nev Harris.

A planted aviary with multiple flights and landscaped gardens owned by Gus Margetts.

Provision of a hide in a colony aviary is recommended for the more private inhabitants.

Colony Housing

Housing finches in a colony is a common practice and an excellent way to provide both an interesting and aesthetic addition to your backyard. However, if you are actively propagating a variety or line breeding birds for specific characteristics, the community environment does not provide a means of controlling the genetic base with which you are working. In colony breeding there is no inexpensive method of determining unequivocally the parentage of young from a specific nest (apart from DNA paternity testing). Another point to consider is that levels of aggression are often high in colony situations. Housing pairs of Gouldian Finches separately reduces this problem dramatically.

However, many aviculturists prefer the colony breeding system and while it may not be as selective as individual cage breeding, good quality birds can be produced if the aviculturist selects the breeding stock carefully. If size and colour are the criteria then all the birds in the colony should be selected with that in mind. Ideally Gouldian Finches should be colony housed as a single species, preferably according to head colour.

The number of pairs in a breeding colony should be commensurate with the size of the aviary. By setting up more pairs in order to produce more youngsters, the problem of overcrowding is created, which in turn causes stress. Birds that are under stress are more likely to contract a bacterial infection because of their lowered resistance. In fact, instead of producing more youngsters the breeder is more likely to finish up with fewer youngsters being bred. Birds which are inferior should not be selected for breeding. Improvement is gradual and may take several generations to achieve.

Susceptibility to the Effects of Cold and Wet Conditions

Temperatures are warm to hot in the natural tropical range of the Gouldian Finch where, unlike other Australian finches, they thrive during the extreme summer heat. Other Australian finches wilt as the temperatures rise above 35°C but Gouldian Finches are best at these high temperatures and enjoy bathing in the direct sunshine much more than other finches. Flighted aviaries that capture the morning sun help with health problems and sustain breeding activity into the cooler months of the year. Provisions should also be made for additional shelves and perches to be placed in the open flight area during hot weather for water baths and sunbaking.

Gouldian Finches look dejected and fluff up during wet overcast weather. They breed best in aviaries away from the humidity of the coast, preferring weather conditions of clear skies and hot temperatures that resemble the climate of their natural breeding habitat. Breeding activity is awakened by extended rains that provide grass seeds in numbers to support the rearing of young. The low humidity (dry air), high temperatures and clear skies of the savanna woodlands away from the coastal humidity and rainfall provide these conditions. Breeding problems for captive birds should be expected when similar cloudy, wet conditions prevail. Ornamental aviaries with water displays do not offer the dry environment enjoyed by these finches and they may not breed well under these conditions.

Wild Gouldian Finches (Study Population) at Katherine recovering from a cold night.

Fluctuations in temperature, high humidity and draughts are the main enemy of breeding and juvenile birds. The wild Gouldian Finch is protected from these conditions under the cover of its wooded breeding habitat. They can withstand freezing temperatures in open aviaries as long as they are healthy and protected from draughts, the night-time condensation of moist air and sudden fluctuations in temperature and humidity.

They rarely breed well in cold climates and chick mortality is high. Breeding failures during cold spells are inevitable because they are naturally poor brooders, often leaving their nest in the wild for extended periods especially when temperatures rise above 36°C. Here high daytime temperatures and mild evenings protect their eggs and young. Their innately poor brooding skills expose their clutches of eggs and young to failure during cold weather.

Unlike other Australian finches, juvenile Gouldian Finches (as well as Painted and

Pictorella Finches) roost alone with no physical contact. They are, therefore, more susceptible to the effects of cold and fluctuating temperatures during a time when there is a considerable natural demand for energy resources in weaning, fledging and the juvenile moult.

Housing in Temperate Regions

Housing the Gouldian Finch successfully in cooler climates, especially where temperatures drop below 10°C, requires a purpose-built aviary. This finch enjoys 35°C heat, which does not mean that it likes to be excessively hot. However they will never proliferate if kept in a cold, damp environment.

Providing the correct aviary is paramount to the health of the Gouldian Finch. It must be warm, dry and draught-free and give the birds access to the sun throughout the day. These conditions can be addressed by facing the aviaries north-east (in the Southern Hemisphere) with an unenclosed central section measuring approximately 2.5 metres allowing sun to penetrate the aviary for the entire day. This allows the birds to warm up prior to roosting which appears to improve their survival rate.

Gouldian Finch enthusiasts in northern Australia are lucky in being able to house birds in simple enclosures with a minimum of fuss.

Housing in Tropical Regions

Keeping Gouldian Finches in tropical regions poses particular problems because the weather is dominated by the cycles of the Wet Season and the Dry Season. There is a lot of rain for a few months of the year and no rain for the rest of the year. In tropical regions there is no need to closet Gouldian Finches away from excessively low temperatures. Although temperatures may drop to below 10°C overnight the days are very warm, about 33°C. Birds are able to find the sun quickly and warm their small, chilled bodies. This is evident in the wild. On unusually cold mornings wild Gouldian Finches can be seen perched in the tops of dead trees catching as much sun and warmth as possible. Once they have sunned themselves for a half an hour or more, bringing their bodies up to a reasonable temperature, they fly off to drink and find seed. It is important, therefore, to give your birds the earliest access to the morning sun. However, in the tropics it is even more important for your birds to have somewhere cool to sit during the heat of the day. During the Dry Season daytime temperatures start to climb and in some tropical areas it is not uncommon to experience temperatures of 38°C for several months. As this is also the birds' moulting period it is very important to reduce their exposure to heat stress.

In this climate aviaries can be quite a simple construction—merely a wire flight attached to a sheltered enclosure. Face the front of the aviary in a north-easterly direction to give the birds exposure to the early morning sun while also reducing the length of time subjected to the hot westerly afternoon sun. It is a good idea to position the aviary near or under small trees and shrubs. The dappled shade will reduce temperatures further. An important aspect to consider in a tropical climate is the problem of excessive moisture. During the Wet Season this can cause damp floors and walls which can lead to sooty mould—a serious problem to the good health of the Gouldian Finch. One successful way to combat this problem is to house your birds in suspended cages or flights.

Indoor Housing in Cooler Regions

Gouldian Finches are often housed in indoor cages and cabinets in cooler climates. This type of facility may be artificially heated to reduce temperature fluctuations, may have additional electric lighting, and can be fan-ventilated or airconditioned. Using this system has numerous advantages, including the ability to control the length of the breeding season and reduce the incidence of egg binding during unseasonally cold periods. Unfortunately, if this type of housing is not managed correctly there can be some disadvantages. Birds may not experience sufficient seasonal temperature variations which could lead to a prolonged moult and poor synchronisation of nesting within a colony. There may also be problems with production of vitamin D3 through lack of direct sunlight. If the room is not designed appropriately, with sufficient ventilation, the air may become stale and the birds may appear lethargic.

Housing Structures

Conventional Aviaries

The conventional aviary of the twenty-first century consists of an outdoor flight attached to a shelter. For many enthusiasts it is also important to take into account the aesthetics of the aviary as well as its functionality. As with other designs, the aviary should be positioned to receive early morning sun and be in easy view for the aviculturist to adequately monitor the birds' activities. An ideal structure should measure approximately 3 metres long x 1 metre wide x 2.1 metres high, with at least half the aviary fully enclosed.

Construction using (25mm x 25mm) steel tubing and 5mm x 5mm wire is the most robust, especially for the flight which is exposed to the weather. The flight should have plenty of room to allow the birds to 'stretch their wings' as well as space for perches and water receptacles. Perches should be positioned away from food and water bowls to prevent fouling and not too close to the aviary walls. This is most important because

Above: Aviary complex.

Right: This aviary complex incorporates a half-open, half-sheltered design. A flap door can completely enclose the birds in the sheltered area.

Inset: The flap door set-up designed by John Sammut.

Inside an aviary complex.

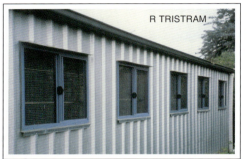
The windows in this enclosed aviary complex provide the birds with access to direct sunlight and fresh air.

Conventional aviary complex.

predators such as goshawks often hit the wire as they swoop to attack your birds. If the aviary occupants are perched too close to the wire they are more likely to die from shock.

Depending on the climate, the shelter should be lined and insulated if possible. The provision of a flap door on the front of this section can, when shut, fully enclose the area, protecting the birds from inclement weather. Nestboxes, seed receptacles and additional perches for roosting should be located in the shelter. A safety area at the rear of the aviary should include external access to feed stations and nestboxes and an entry into the aviary.

Floors are usually either concrete or dirt. If dirt is the option then appropriate footings to support the structure and to aid the prevention of rodent entry should be put into place prior to construction. The aviary base should have brick or cement footings rising approximately 15cm above ground level. A sheet metal apron 40cm high around the perimeter of the base will prevent rodent entry. If snakes are a problem the apron should measure 1.2 metres high. Rodents are also deterred if a concrete path is placed around the entire aviary, butting directly to the walls.

The aviary design should take into account the basic housing requirements for Gouldian Finches—minimal exposure to draughts, inclement weather and excess moisture, prevention of rodent entry and the degree of sun penetration depending on climatic conditions. In general the principles of construction described for other enclosures are the same, the only difference being the less specialised nature of the final product.

Note the safety door into the storage and quarantine area.

Suspended aviary used by Milton Lewis to successfully house and breed Gouldian Finches.

Suspended aviaries allow debris to fall through to a catching area below.

Suspended Cages and Aviaries

The major benefit of suspended housing is that of easier hygiene maintenance. These cages have been more fully utilised overseas, possibly because Australian backyards have had ample space to construct large aviaries. However in recent years it has become more popular to house a larger number of birds in a smaller area.

A suspended cage is quite simply a partially enclosed, rectangular structure raised above the ground. The floor is constructed of wire, allowing food debris and faeces to fall through the bottom of the cage onto the ground or onto collecting trays. In the past this system has been employed for small wire cabinets that are often stacked one upon the other to create a bank somewhat similar to the cabinets used by canary enthusiasts.

However the concept can also be adapted to create large, suspended free-standing aviaries. This is particularly useful for bird keepers who move house. The aviary can be quickly disassembled and erected again without the need for constructing a new floor. These aviaries are also very useful for those bird keepers living in rented accommodation, because they can be built above an existing garden or lawn, without destroying or altering it.

The greatest advantage is the ease with which these systems can be cleaned. In the case of small cages, the collecting tray is simply removed, emptied and a new layer of paper or sand added to absorb the faeces. This cleaning process can be performed whenever necessary with minimal fuss to either the birds or the keeper. Aviaries with a wire floor can be cleaned with a hose to wash off the accumulation of faeces on the wire.

Cabinet and Cage Breeding

In Australia breeding Gouldian Finches in cabinets is not widely practised. The weather by and large is favourable and building an aviary in a backyard is easier and cheaper than building a birdroom for cage breeding. However some aviculturists may prefer to use this system for selective mutation breeding purposes.

The size of the cage is of no great importance, as long as the birds feel secure. A box-type cage with a wire front should be at least 45cm deep. Height and width could be varied but a cage measuring 90cm long x 60cm high should provide enough room for a pair of birds.

If housed indoors, birds need to receive sufficient full-spectrum UV lighting to maintain good health and breeding success.

A bank of indoor cabinets.

Two perches are placed as far apart from each other as possible, but not too close to the ends of the cage otherwise the cock's tail feathers will be damaged. Some breeders place the perches diagonally opposite each other. They maintain that such an arrangement gives the birds more exercise by making them fly up to the top perch. Perches measuring 10mm thick can be roughened by dragging a fine-toothed saw along them.

The wire front must have enough openings to accommodate a nestbox, seed and water containers, a softfood container, a clip to hold cuttlefish bone and an opening sufficiently large enough to catch the birds— a small net 15–20cm in diameter is handy for this purpose. A container with mineralised grit hung on the inside of the cage front will complete the set-up. It must be mentioned that experiments in relocating cabinet-bred birds to an aviary environment have not been successful in the long term. This is possibly due to the differing energy levels required in such opposite environments. This would apply in particular to weaker families of finches.

Holding Cages

One area that is often overlooked is the need to have adequate space to accommodate newly fledged birds. This is a critical time in the life of young birds as they need to feel comfortable and be given maximum time to develop and grow. It is easy to fill cages with birds capable of breeding and neglect the accommodation needs of their fledglings. When planning your aviary set-up, ensure that you allow for a flight or two for young birds. Leaving newly fledged, young birds with their parents for an excessive time will lead to losses, as the parent birds may wish to resume breeding activities. The development of newly fledged Gouldian Finches requires a flight area of at least 3 metres in length. This will provide them with adequate room to exercise.

Building Materials

When choosing building materials a number of factors should be considered: the functionality of the aviary; the health of the birds; and preventing vermin and predators from gaining access.

Possibly the best option for framing is 25mm x 25mm galvanised steel tubing or sheeting. The structure can be assembled using self-tapping screw rivets or plastic joiners. This is preferable to timber because it is durable and requires limited maintenance. A suitable wall cladding is 7mm plywood. Once painted it is both durable and relatively cheap compared to metal cladding. This can also be coupled with 25mm styrofoam (or an equivalent insulating material) in the walls to prevent sudden temperature changes. The roof of the shelter should be insulated corrugated steel.

Standard galvanised wire mesh is usually 10mm x 10mm but unfortunately this size will still allow access by rodents and even some snakes. It is recommended that 5mm x 5mm wire mesh be used for all external flight surfaces to prevent this problem. Galvanised wire mesh should be washed in a weak solution of vinegar (acetic acid) prior to installation. This will protect the birds from heavy metal poisoning.

Substrate

Floors may be concrete or soil. Dirt floors are a poor choice because they provide reservoirs for parasites. Bare concrete floors are hygienic if kept free of faeces. If concrete floors are covered with fine sand or sawdust, this may compromise hygiene.

These coverings also form reservoirs for parasites because they hold moisture, reducing the likelihood of parasite eggs dying from desiccation. They also promote the growth of mould which is particularly dangerous for Gouldian Finches. A fresh covering of sand or sawdust is aesthetically pleasing, but if the absorptive material is not cleaned or replaced regularly, unnecessary ill health in your valuable breeding stock will result.

Floors consisting of a bed of stones, coarse sand, gravel, grit or diatomaceous earth will provide better drainage and reduce moisture levels and parasite transmission and are worthy of consideration. Suspended floors, of course, have the potential to be the most hygienic if careful attention is given to removing faecal build-up from the wire, especially underneath perches and around seed dishes.

Nesting Receptacles

In general it appears that Gouldian Finches prefer closed nestboxes rather than receptacles like wire baskets. There are several general designs for nestboxes. The first is often referred to as a half-open box, so named because the front of the box is half open. This design is generally not preferred by Gouldians, although it is used by other parrotfinches. The second nestbox, more common in Australia, is preferred. It is accessed through a small round hole (with a 45mm diameter) in the front of the box. Both nestboxes measure approximately 15–18cm long x 12cm wide x 12cm high. A short dowel perch is usually provided at the front of each nestbox.

Nestbox showing chicks amongst the nesting material.

Nestboxes used by breeding Gouldian Finches.

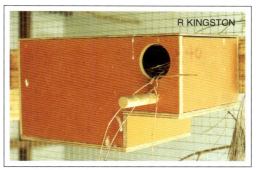

An ideal Gouldian Finch nestbox.

A variety of nestboxes need to be provided in a colony aviary.

Hollow logs can also be provided as a nesting structure.

Gouldian Finches will also nest in natural cavities, eg small hollow logs and in nestboxes with a piece of hollow branch on the front. Twin-compartment nestboxes are also very useful and appear to reduce the incidence of fledglings leaving the nest too early. A hinged nestbox lid allows nest inspection.

Feed Stations

Seed stations, as well as containers for grit, eggshells, salt lick and charcoal, can be located on shelving about halfway between the floor and the ceiling away from perches to minimise faecal contamination. A strip of galvanised metal placed above these food areas will also help prevent contamination. Funnels positioned under water stations will remove surplus water from the aviary with a concrete floor. This can be accomplished by drilling 3cm holes in the concrete slab and running 3cm tubing from the funnel through the aviary floor.

One of the many successful nestbox designs currently in use in Australian aviaries. This design is particularly effective in reducing the number of young lost through being 'kicked out'.

The installation of feed and water stations with external access will reduce the time spent feeding the birds and provide easy removal of dishes for cleaning every day. It also addresses the problem of disturbing the birds to enter the aviary. Cleaning time will be dramatically reduced if seed husks are caught in a plastic bin placed under the feed station. If the perimeter of the feed station has higher sides this will also assist in catching discarded foods. The absence of seed husks and surplus water in the aviary environment also helps control disease. Feed stations can be as large as 1.5 metres long x 70cm high x 70cm deep. While installation costs can be high, the advantages make it worthy of consideration.

In smaller cabinets, tubes, fonts or Budgerigar-type cage containers can be used to provide seed and water. Food and water containers should be no deeper than 25mm.

Feed station in Ron Tristram's aviaries. Seed husks drop into half a 150mm PVC pipe to reduce pollution and cleaning time.

External feed station at Gerard Abrams' aviary set-up. The value of this easily accessed feed station is that it reduces intrusions and pollution caused by seed husks and surplus water. It saves time in feeding and watering and provides easy access.

Water

Gouldian Finches appear to show a distinct preference for rainwater, which is naturally soft. Many aviculturists consider it beneficial to provide their birds with access to rainwater. This can be achieved by having partly unroofed flights where finches are able to gain direct access to rain. Gouldian Finches are also great weather forecasters. Whenever you see the birds roosting in the open flight area at dusk, with their beaks pointing skywards, you can expect rain.

Automated water systems allow for reduced maintenance time.

Rainwater can also be collected in a tank. The installation of a fibreglass tank will ensure that the water properties are not altered during storage and the problem of rust associated with galvanised tanks is avoided. If you are using town supply water the use of filters has merit, as substances such as fluoride, can be removed.

The use of automatic water facilities is recommended and can comprise a coarse and a fine filter coupled to a Nylex™ water computer that turns water on for one minute each day. This is sufficient time to completely change the water in dishes with a 22cm diameter.

All water dishes should be located to minimise faecal contamination and be thoroughly cleaned every 2–3 days.

Perches

Perches should be natural branches of varying thicknesses. These will exercise your birds' feet and possibly prevent a problem called 'claw feet'. Adequate perching should be supplied to prevent fighting over available nesting and roosting sites. In roosting areas of aviaries used to hold large numbers of non-breeding birds individual perches can be beneficial in reducing feather plucking and bullying. Such a perching arrangement can be achieved by using perches 10cm long, either glued to the walls or placed through the wire. Another method of providing individual perch space has been well used in Europe and incorporates a system of small dividers. This very successful system uses long perches onto which small wooden panels or dividers are threaded at a distance equivalent to approximately 1.5 bird-body widths. This is particularly useful when housing larger groups of juveniles during the stressful moulting period.

Natural branch perches will provide exercise for the feet.

Temperature and Humidity Control

In the housing of Gouldian Finches the temperature is particularly relevant. Artificially heated environments can reduce stress caused through excessive temperature variations. However the cooling of aviaries or birdrooms during periods of excessive heat is equally important.

The correct temperature at which Gouldians should be kept is always vigorously debated. However, suffice it to say that if we are going to emulate the conditions of their natural habitat, then winter is, in many areas, somewhat colder than what they should be subjected to.

Most fanciers who breed Gouldian Finches indoors maintain an inside temperature of approximately 18°C at the start of the breeding season. This is a compromise compared to the temperatures experienced in the wild, where minimum temperatures across the breeding habitat range from 12–18°C in July (their coldest month) and maximum temperatures (the start of the breeding season) rise to a range of 30–36°C.

Mutations appear to require much higher temperatures for successful breeding and survival. Mutations must be kept at temperatures above 18°C degrees with some breeders suggesting temperatures as high as 30–36°C for continued breeding. They are unable to maintain their body heat and lose body condition when temperatures drop below 12°C for a prolonged length of time. Thermostatically controlled heaters should provide the best conditions for rearing mutations.

A light bulb located under the nestbox can be used on cold winter nights.

Although artificial heating does improve breeding activity the birds must also receive plenty of sunlight or additional ultraviolet light. Artificial lighting and heating used by mutation enthusiasts for breeding indoors and in cabinets can improve breeding likelihood and the survival chances of newly hatched birds in cold winters. Up to 15 hours of daylight should be provided because breeding Gouldian Finches may not receive enough rest with longer periods of time. Automatic timers are used to switch the light on at 5.00am and off at 6.00pm. A second source of low intensity light, the night-light, should come on 15 minutes beforehand. Its dimming effect prevents plunging the birds into sudden darkness at night and provides a gradual build-up to daylight in the morning.

The humidity during the breeding season should be kept within the range of 55–70%. Maintaining the humidity at the lower end of this range minimises the development of pathogens within the breeding room. However, it is also very important to have sufficient humidity at the time of hatching.

Heat pads have been used on nestboxes in colder regions and are probably very effective in safeguarding against losses during unseasonably cold conditions. Some fanciers believe that heat pads, like other artificial aids, promote the breeding of birds that would normally not survive but this is an individual decision. The use of 25W light bulbs or porcelain bulbs in the roosting area, to alleviate these cold conditions, is also worth consideration.

Human Disturbance

Entering the aviary to perform general maintenance or nest inspections could be detrimental to your birds and reduce breeding success. Although Gouldian Finches do not normally object to nest inspections, these should be kept to a minimum, as some birds have been known to abandon a nest immediately afterwards while others may throw the young out of the nest if they feel threatened by the intrusion. The presence of a human in the aviary can also startle the birds, causing them to collide with the walls.

Installing external feed stations is one way of reducing the time spent in the aviary. Aviculturists who have installed external feeding stations report a reduction in the loss of both parent birds and young.

Transportation

When catching birds in an aviary, ensure that the net is soft enough to cushion the impact and that the material (eg mosquito net) has small holes to minimise leg damage.

It is good practice to pad the wire edging of the net to lessen the impact should it come in contact with the bird.

Gouldian Finches do not travel well and special arrangements need to be made prior to the relocation as well as on arrival at a destination. The week prior to transportation, acclimatise the birds to a carry box measuring 1.2 metres long x 50cm high x 30cm deep. Increase their electrolyte levels, as the birds may become stressed when moved from their aviary environment. Relocate birds in the morning to allow them time to settle, find food supplies and roosting areas in their new aviary.

Carry Boxes

Carry boxes used to transport Gouldian Finches over long distances must be well designed to reduce the incidence of stress and injuries. Birds may damage their head feathers if the box height is too small. A box with a height of 15cm addresses this problem and does not cause the birds to crouch when being transported. It is also important to limit the area of wire on the front of the box. This area should only be big enough to allow in some light for the birds to find seed and water. Large, open fronts increase the likelihood of birds being scared by movement outside the box and also expose birds to draughts when boxes are sitting in air cargo sheds prior to being placed within cargoholds. A hinged or sliding front with adequate ventilation is beneficial. Overcrowding must be avoided.

A well-designed carry box with individual compartments can transport a number of birds at the one time.

Supply a sprinkling of seed on the cage floor and if travelling over long distances, add to the carry box a small plastic container with a piece of cotton wool soaked in water. This will provide the bird with adequate water without making a mess on the floor of the carry box.

Do not transport your birds in the boot of the car. Exhaust fumes from the car will find their way into the boot with disastrous results. Do not leave the carry box in a locked car in the sun. The rapid rise in temperature will kill the birds. Do not place the carry box on the passenger seat without first securing it into position, as sudden braking will cause the box to tip over with possible injuries to its occupants.

Quarantine

Newly acquired birds should be held in quarantine for 3–6 weeks in a holding cage. This allows you to monitor the health of the birds and observe closely how well the birds are acclimatising to their new environment. Use newspaper on the floor of the cage to monitor digestion and to collect faeces for veterinary analysis. You must be aware of environmental changes and be prepared to help the birds acclimatise. If the birds' environment changes from say, a dry, hot area to a humid, hot area, there is an increased risk that the birds will be affected by Coccidiosis.

You should also:
- Maintain the diet the birds have been used to.
- Supply fresh boiled water for the first few days.
- Introduce new foods gradually to prevent overfeeding and digestion problems.
- Elevate seed and water containers so that they are easily accessible.
- Locate the cage in a quiet, warm location with minimal disturbance for the first few days.
- Provide your veterinarian with dropping samples for health analysis.

NUTRITION

A group of Gouldian Finches feeding on seed sprays in the collection of Bob Buckley.

Introduction

Nutrition is vital to successful breeding and the correct balance must be provided. In evolutionary terms, the protein quantity required during breeding appears to be less for Estrildinae grassfinches than other birds in the wild. Half-ripe seeds provide most finches with enough protein quality and quantity to breed in good numbers. In the wild the dietary requirements vary between finch species. These special needs must also be met in captivity.

The captive diet of the Gouldian Finch can be complex and seems to vary greatly amongst aviculturists. The food equation must be balanced. Gouldian Finches will benefit from more protein and nutritional supplements in their food during the moult, when breeding or when fresh foods are not provided. The need for nutritional supplementation decreases proportionately to the amount of sunlight, fresh air and fresh foods—seeding grasses, greenfoods, eggs and vegetables—they receive as well as their fitness and inherent health.

Wonderful examples of healthy Yellow-headed Normal Gouldian Finches.

The more delicate Gouldian Finch mutations require a more exacting level of nutrition during the breeding season than Normal Gouldians. Greater amounts of protein, vitamins, minerals and energy must be given to these birds to achieve comparable breeding results. Weak strains, especially the Blue varieties, are significantly advantaged when nutritionally rich softfoods are added to their diet during the breeding and moult seasons. Knowledge of the nutritional requirements is the foundation of breeding success.

Protein

Proteins are vital for the overall growth of the bird. Muscles, eyes, skin, feathers and nervous system, all require protein for their proper development and growth. Proteins are made up of various amino acids, with lysine and methionine being the major breeding proteins.

In captivity, it is not possible to provide the variety of seeds and seeding grasses required to balance the protein needs of breeding finches. Therefore additional sources of protein must be provided. Soaked and 'just-sprouted' 'oil' seeds, such as niger and rape, are rich in protein and carbohydrates while 'starch' seeds, including canary and millets, are rich in carbohydrates but lower in protein.

Minerals

Minerals, like vitamins, are an essential part of the diet. For example, calcium is taken in great quantity by the egg-laying Gouldian Finch hen for eggshell formation while phosphorus and calcium together are vital for bone formation.

Additional minerals and trace elements must be given to breeding birds because dry seeds are a very poor source of these. Calcium, phosphorous, iodine, iron, zinc, sodium and chloride are the most important minerals that birds need for continuing good health. Minerals and trace elements, the most neglected part of good nutrition for breeding birds, should be made available at all times. Commercial mineral supplements such as Tracemin™ are readily available.

Grit

Grit is a method of supplying minerals and important for the efficient functioning of the crop. The regular grits contain calcium but are deficient in iodine, iron and most trace elements. Mineralised grit is required to provide breeding flocks with the mineral

TABLE 1
PERCENTAGE COMPARISON OF BASIC NUTRITIONAL COMPONENTS IN COMMONLY USED FOODS FOR GOULDIAN FINCHES

FOOD ITEM	PROTEIN	FAT	CARBO-HYDRATE	FIBRE	MOISTURE	ASH
White Millet	11.8	4.0	59.9	8.0	12.0	4.3
Japanese Millet	12.6	4.8	60.8	8.6	11.5	3.7
Canary	15.2	5.4	57.7	5.1	11.5	5.1
Panicum	10.9	2.9	55.2	14.3	12.8	3.9
Niger	18.9	37.1	19.2	9.8	8.0	7.0
Linseed	18.2	38.6	20.0	12.1	7.9	3.2
Rape	19.3	45.0	17.6	5.9	8.0	4.2
High Protein Baby Cereal	19.0	5.5	58.1	–	–	–
Egg (hard-boiled)	12.5	11.6	0.7	–	–	–
Foxtail Millet (fresh)	9.6	3.21	–	31.8	–	8.9
Foxtail Millet (grain)	13.6	4.6	–	9.3	–	4.0
Wheat	14.4	1.8	3.7	2.8	–	–
Groats	17.6	6.9	3.6	2.8	–	2.3

Data sourced from Leaney et al (1993), Kingston (1994) and Wildlife Conservation Society (pers. comm.)

and trace element requirements. Very fine (1mm), dry shell grit mixed with finely crushed charcoal and eggshells is best suited for Gouldian Finches. Outbreaks of obstruction-related deaths may occur when cold or wet conditions cause feeding parents to overeat grit. Small-sized grit is less likely to result in these outbreaks.

Charcoal.

Mineralised grit.

Vitamins

Vitamins are required in only small amounts, nevertheless they are essential. Vitamin A is a particularly important vitamin for birds. It promotes appetite, increases resistance to infection and aids digestion. Deficiency can lead to sterility, retarded growth and blindness. The signs of a deficiency are subtle, but are exhibited in the condition of the feather and its colour intensity. Birds with a vitamin A deficiency have pale, rough and dull feathers.

All of the B vitamins, especially thiamine, help accelerate the recovery of ill birds by reducing stress. The vitamins A, D and E stimulate and restore the metabolism after a bout of illness.

White millet heads are fed in winter to provide fresh green seed.

Vitamin supplements must be added to the drinking water once a week because dry seed alone cannot provide the balance or levels of vitamins needed for breeding good quality and healthy young. Seed mixes lack vitamins A, D, E and are low in vitamin B. Half-ripe seeding grasses do, however, contain much greater levels of these vitamins. Partially open flights are recommended for all finches because direct sunlight is by far the best source of vitamin D—essential for good fertility and strong eggs.

Carbohydrates

Carbohydrates provide the primary sources of energy to keep body warmth through their breakdown and supply of energy to all the functioning parts of the bird's body. It is almost impossible for a deficiency in carbohydrates to arise if the seed mix includes canary seed, French white, Japanese and Hungarian (panicum) millets which are very rich in carbohydrates.

The importance of providing additional energy during breeding has not previously been a topic of great interest but should be addressed by all finch breeders. As well as vitamins, minerals and trace elements, additional energy is also required for successful breeding performance and good health. Energy is a most necessary ingredient for breeding success because of the extremely high metabolic rate and the small size of finches. Energy must be provided to captive finches to raise their young. The feeding of soaked seed to breeding parents with young provides chicks with an instant source of energy. When germinating seeds the starch is transformed into glucose and this in turn is more readily absorbed into the bird's digestive system.

Carbohydrates, fats and protein are all sources of energy and half-ripe seeding grasses are a most reliable source. Wild finches rely upon their presence for the extreme levels of energy required to breed and rear young.

Breeding birds use many times more energy than non-breeding birds and above all, it is the energy content of the food that determines breeding success or failure. Certainly the quality of protein is important, but often too much attention has been placed upon the protein content of the food and not enough on energy.

Fats

Fats offer the most efficient conversion to energy but finch species cannot tolerate high levels of oil in their diet. Excess fats are stored in the body.

Nutritional Supplements

Over the years, many methods and recipes have been devised to provide captive Gouldian Finches and other grassfinches with a good breeding diet but with varying degrees of success. Many of the gaps in knowledge of bird nutrition have been filled but some remain. We are now better able to provide a more precise level of nutrition to breeding birds. High quality nutritional supplements that may be added to the drinking water or the softfood mix or as a dry edible powder are available. These ensure that the best nutritional balance is met for those finch keepers unwilling, unable or do not have the time to provide fresh grasses and foods each day.

Nutritional supplements must be given to all captive finches, especially Gouldian Finch mutations, because their enclosed environment cannot provide them with the variety of nutrients required for breeding success. Seeds and seeding grasses on their own do not provide the nutritional diversity required for sustained breeding activity in captive finches.

Dietary Cycles

The energy and growth needs of Gouldian Finches must be understood if you wish to breed them successfully. The Gouldian Finch life cycle can be considered as annual, with a number of important metabolic events occurring within this period. It is useful to understand which events require special dietary consideration.

In the wild, Gouldian Finches are subjected to periods of naturally low food availability as well as periods of metabolic stress. Food availability depends on the seasons. Therefore, for a short period during the Wet Season there is an abundant supply of fresh, half-ripe and ripe seed. For the rest of the year only dry seed is obtainable from the ground. These seeds form the staple diet for young born after April as well as for adults throughout the Dry Season.

At the end of the Dry Season Gouldian Finches face their most difficult metabolic challenge with the onset of the moult. The next period of metabolic stress is prior to and during breeding when adults require both protein and extra sources of carbohydrates as energy. In order to house and breed Gouldian Finches adequately it is vitally important to understand these events and provide suitable resources to enable the finches to survive and thrive.

Moult Diet

The moult is at its height during November and December, but sometimes extends into February (in the Southern Hemisphere). This is the most stressful period in the annual life cycle of the Gouldian Finch.

The diet must be a priority at this time if the death of large numbers of juvenile Gouldian Finches is to be avoided. During the moult both adults and juveniles completely renew all their feathers. The new tissue in these feathers requires extra protein and building these feathers requires energy. Therefore seed mixes must not only be nutritionally balanced but also contain easily metabolised forms of both carbohydrates and protein. (See *Table 2*.)

When offered a selection of seeds it is interesting to note that moulting birds tend to select canary seed and then supplement this with French white millet. As a result it is suggested that an extra portion of canary seed be added to the seed mix during the moulting period and then removed as the moult finishes.

Approximately twice a week during this period provide some supplementation in the form of sprouted seed and egg or softfoods. This supplementation must cease as soon as the moult is complete because the birds may become fat and die. Exercise and a continuous supply of greenfood are also vital during this period. Some of the recommended greenfoods readily available at this time of the year are endive, chicory and bok choy. However the choice of greenfood does not seem to matter a great deal as long as it is supplied daily.

Non-breeding Diet

In the non-breeding season when the birds are out of the moult, supply a dry mix which consists of canary, French white millet, Japanese millet and Hungarian (Panicum) millet, cuttlefish bone and mineralised grit. (See *Table 2*.) The above mix should always be available and form the staple diet throughout the year. The four types of seeds fed are also very rich in carbohydrates. Vitamins are supplied in the water 2–3 times weekly. Greenfood, such as chickweed, can be given about every second day. Seeding grasses are highly nutritious if one can obtain them regularly. The cultivation of your own seeding grasses and greenfood will ensure a regular, uncontaminated supply.

Pre-breeding Diet

The pre-breeding diet should be used for approximately six weeks prior to pairing birds for breeding. Prior to breeding, Gouldian Finches should be lean and in good condition. This can be achieved by controlling what they eat and providing them with space to exercise. Gouldian Finches can be stimulated to breed by the introduction of seeding grasses and protein-rich food sources, such as sprouted or soaked seed that contain the essential breeding amino acids lysine and methionine.

Grass seeds form a large part of the wild bird's diet. In the weeks before the commencement of the breeding season the basic diet is supplemented with a pre-breeding mix of niger, rape and lettuce seed, as

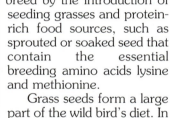

Pit Pit Grass, grown in the Brisbane area, is used during the breeding season. Above right: Close-up of Pit Pit Grass.

Left: Green Panic, a seed often grown by Gouldian breeders in the Brisbane area, is very useful as a dietary supplement. Centre: Saltbush is a favourite of Gouldian Finches and is now grown widely as a dietary supplement. Right: Chickweed is a favourite greenfood.

well as a small amount of wild Phalaris grass seed which is relished by the birds. (See Table 2.) At this time Gouldian Finches require large quantities of fresh seeding grasses daily, including umbrella grass, winter grass, green and purple swamp grass (also known as green panic), chickweed, wild oats and dock. These grasses belong to genera including *Poa, Digitaria, Eriochloa, Panicum* and *Pennisetum*. The supply of fresh, French white millet heads is important. They are high in seed milk and more readily absorbed into the young birds' digestive system than greenfood.

Breeding Diet

Breeding commences in March or April (in the Southern Hemisphere), depending on the condition of the birds and the region where they are housed. At this time the diet must contain sufficient carbohydrates to sustain the added activities of the adults when feeding the young. The diet should also be rich in proteins to promote egg production in the hens and growth in the nestlings.

Frozen half-ripe millet heads.

During breeding it has been observed that Gouldian Finches eat more French white millet in preference to other seeds—greater amounts can be added to the diet as required. Table 2 contains an example of a proven Gouldian Finch seed mix suitable for the breeding season. Provide greenfoods such as endive daily, as well as millet sprays and fresh seeding grasses in season. To ensure a constant supply of these grasses during the breeding season, which coincides with winter in the Southern Hemisphere, it is important to plan ahead. This can be done by harvesting grass and millet heads throughout the growing season and storing bunches in the freezer. The frozen grass can be used daily throughout the winter months. A protein and carbohydrate rich diet should include soaked seeds, softfoods and sprouted seeds.

Softfoods, Soaked and Sprouted Seeds

The prime objective of any softfood, soaked or sprouted seed recipe must be to provide the breeding birds with an extra source of quality protein and energy. As well as an increased need for energy and protein during breeding, finches also need extra vitamins, trace elements and minerals. Softfoods and soaked or sprouted seed offer an

Table 2
Percentage Composition of Dry Seed Mixes Recommended During the Life Cycle of the Gouldian Finch

SEED	MOULT	NON-BREEDING	PRE-BREEDING	BREEDING
French Millet	25	25	15	10
Hungarian Millet	5	25	15	10
Japanese Millet	10	25	15	10
Red Millet	5	–	15	10
Canary	45	25	20	40
Groats	–	–	–	10
Wheat	–	–	–	5
Niger	5	–	5	2
Rape	–	–	5	3
Phalaris	–	–	5	–
Lettuce	–	–	5	–

Sprouted seed mixes can be fed throughout the breeding season.

excellent vehicle by which vitamins, trace elements and minerals can be administered. Without these additional supplements, breeding birds tire easily and do not feed their young vigorously. The result is weak or dead chicks and sick parents.

Finch breeders have developed various softfood, soaked and sprouted seed recipes. These recipes have been very successful but are often complex, requiring time and special care to prepare. With current scientific knowledge, these recipes can now be simplified by using nutritional supplements. These have been developed to provide the additional protein and energy, as well as vitamin, mineral and trace element requirements for breeding success in a convenient and hygienic form. They can be added to softfood, soaked seed or combined softfood/soaked seed recipes with equal success.

Softfoods

In the wild, insects and protein-rich seeds provide finches with the protein required for breeding. In the past, various egg food (now known as softfood) recipes have traditionally been used to provide additional protein. With improved knowledge of finch nutrition, it is possible to make a simple and effective softfood recipe. 'Green' half-ripe seeds relished by wild finches, soaked seed or individual dry seeds are used as the starting-point ingredients to a softfood recipe. Additional nutrients can then be added according to the individual preference of the enthusiast. From a nutritional point of view the softfood recipes must contain both protein and carbohydrates for the feeding parents.

The Normal Gouldian Finch may breed without the addition of protein to the diet. However, Gouldian mutations must be provided with additional protein to breed successfully. The addition of vitamins, minerals and trace elements to softfood recipes completes the nutritional needs of all breeding finches.

Softfoods also provide sick finches with a palatable and highly nutritious form of energy that promotes and accelerates recovery.

Softfood Mix

- 12 hard-boiled eggs (minimum of 25 minutes cooking time)
- 250 grams rice cereal
- 100 grams chicken starter pellets
- 50 grams coarse ground seed (equal quantities niger, lettuce, French white millet, canary and red millet seeds)
- 30 grams probiotic powder

The eggs are mashed and mixed with the ground rice cereal and starter pellets. The seed and the probiotic powder are then folded into the mixture. This is then bagged in daily portions and frozen until required. On the morning that it is fed to birds it is heated in a microwave for a few seconds. Any uneaten softfood should be discarded the same day.

Soaked and Sprouted Seed

The popular process of feeding soaked or sprouted seed to aviary finches provides the chicks with protein and more importantly an instant source of energy. This concentrated form of energy is a good means of improving breeding success and producing robust and healthy chicks.

Soaked and sprouted seeds provide instant energy during every part of the breeding cycle—courtship, nest making, egg laying, incubating and feeding.

It is possible to design a soaked or sprouted seed mix that provides a good balance of protein for growing chicks. The protein balance refers to the ratio of essential amino acids in the seed mix. For the best growth rate and breeding results all of these must be provided in the correct balance. To achieve this aim it is necessary to calculate the amino acid content of each seed type and then design a mix that balances the amino acid requirements. Lysine and methionine are the most difficult amino acids to balance because they are not found in many seeds. These are known as the 'breeding amino acids' because of their importance for breeding success. Lysine is found in groats, wheat and rape. Sunflower and safflower are rich sources of both lysine and methionine. Groats, rape, wheat, sunflower and safflower are therefore the best 'protein' seeds for sprouting. Millets and plain canary seed are very low in these two important amino acids but are high in energy. They may be sprouted for energy but not as a protein source.

The seed selected for soaking or sprouting must be pre-tested for cleanliness by culture testing or sprouting on cotton wool. Seed that bubbles excessively, smells bad or grows fungus must be rejected. For safety no more than three seed types, preferably sunflower, rape and wheat, should be chosen for sprouting. Uneaten remnants should be removed within six hours. Alternatives to soaked seed should be considered when the quality of the seed is unknown because of its potential danger to growing chicks.

When seed is soaked in warm water the germinating process transforms the starch inside the seeds into a sweet form of immediate energy. The warmth and moisture changes the sour taste of the starch into the sweet taste of a simple sugar that the breeding birds love so much. Both the growing chicks and parents thrive, because the energy requirements (nine times higher during breeding) are satisfied rapidly. The feeding process is a very physically demanding process for the parents and the instant energy provided by soaked and sprouted seed allows them to rear clutches without tiring.

Pairs of healthy Red-headed Normal Gouldian Finches.

Many breeders also mix egg food with soaked or sprouted seed. This is relished by breeding Gouldian Finches.

Unfortunately the potential dangers of contamination may outweigh the benefits of using soaked and sprouted seed, unless stringent hygiene is practised throughout the soaking and sprouting process. Soaked and sprouted seed can become contaminated with mould and bacteria which may seriously hinder the success of the breeding season and cause the loss of both adult and young Gouldian Finches. Poor soaking and sprouting technique is the cause of *E. coli* related chick deaths. Softfoods that do not include soaked seeds and incorporate vitamin/mineral supplements provide a good alternative to the potential contamination problems associated with soaked seed.

Soaked Seed Process

- Soak the clean seed overnight in a solution containing disinfectant, eg Aviclens™, and water in a ratio of 1:100.
- Rinse the seed thoroughly several times until the water runs clear.
- Soak the seed for a further 10–12 minutes in a solution of bleach or disinfectant, eg Aviclens™, and water at a ratio of 1:100.
- Rinse again several times in water before feeding to your birds.
- Any uneaten soaked seed should be discarded daily.

Sprouted Seed Process
- Soak the clean seed overnight in a solution containing disinfectant, eg Aviclens™, and water in a ratio of 1:100.
- Rinse the seed thoroughly several times until the water runs clear.
- Place the seed in a sieve and leave in a warm place.
- Wash the seed thoroughly twice daily in a solution of bleach or disinfectant and water at a ratio of 1:100 until the sprouts appear. Abort the process if the seed has an offensive odour. By day three the sprouted seed should be ready. It is more beneficial to feed the sprouts in the early stages of emerging and not as the shoots turn green.
- Soak the seed for a further 12 minutes in a dilute solution of bleach.
- Rinse thoroughly in water before feeding to the birds.
- Any uneaten sprouted seed must be discarded the same day.

Canary seed.

Rape seed.

Niger seed.

Dry Seed

It is vitally important to provide high quality, fresh clean seed as the *first* step in correct feeding. It is also essential that aviculturists be aware of the protein and carbohydrate content of seed in order to maintain stock in the best condition, especially during the breeding season. (See *Table 1* on page 39.) Clean, fresh seed is essential to a successful breeding season.

Gouldian Finches, like all grassfinches, prefer a seed mix that contains a high variety of small seeds. Knowing the energy content of each seed helps to design a high-energy dry seed mix. Millet varieties, plain canary, groats and rape are high-energy seeds that should be incorporated into the dry seed mix. A dry seed mix may provide the breeding finch with a good source of energy but this is not enough for the chicks to develop quickly in the aviary environment.

It is not advisable to add minerals or vitamins to the seed mix because the salts in mineral powders and shell grits attract moisture that rapidly contaminates grain. Fresh sugar-free vitamins are best administered via the drinking water once a week.

Purchasing Seed

If possible, obtain your seed direct from a grower or at least buy a highly reputable brand. Locally grown seed is generally not heat-treated. Imported seed is heat-treated and also lacks freshness. Some seed growers premix millet seeds when ordered in bulk. This makes life a lot easier as the millets are similar in nutritional content and buying in bulk saves on the storage space that would be required if millet had to be stored according to type.

High quality seed is easily recognised by the size and cleanliness of the grain. Poor quality seed is small and often accompanied by copious quantities of dust and husk. Seeds fed to finches should be low in moisture content to ensure that there is no contamination with mould. As a guide, grains with a moisture content of between 10–12% at the time of harvest are unlikely to be contaminated. Gouldian Finches do not thrive on low-grade seed. It is worth paying more for better quality produce. In Australia, periodic severe drought conditions will result in the importation of large quantities of seed. The purchase of imported seed is best avoided. Imported canary seed, in particular, is of little value to birds and can cost twice the price of locally grown seed.

Culture testing is a good method for checking the quality of grain. Sprouting may also be used to test the cleanliness of seed. Healthy seed gives a 90% sprout rate and has a sweet, fresh smell after 72 hours. Contaminated seed will emit a foul odour and develop a mould growth at between 72–96 hours.

Seed Storage

The correct storage of grain is as important as the purchase of good grain. It is a vital part of maintaining the highest quality of feed for the birds. It must be kept dry, clean and protected from vermin and insects. Seed should be stored in airtight, metal bins. Plastic containers are not rat-proof!

Water

Clean, fresh water must be provided daily. During the breeding season in-water vitamin supplements are recommended once or twice a week. The addition of water cleansers can protect Gouldian Finches from potentially harmful bacteria and assist in the control of disease.

BREEDING

Red-headed Gouldian Finch cock.

Introduction

In the wild, Gouldian Finches breed from February–August, with birds attaining breeding age in their first year of adult plumage. What seems to trigger the Gouldian to breed in the wild is the abundance of seeding grasses which soon appear after the rains. This change seems to awaken their reproductive organs into activity. In the cock it starts with the enlargement of testes which until now have been small and inactive. In the hen the ovaries begin to develop as she comes into breeding condition.

Some breeders pair their birds in early December while others start in late February, depending on the climatic conditions. Under natural conditions breeding activities slow down with the onset of winter. Breeders who use artificial lighting and heating can afford to pair their birds late as they do not appear to be affected by the onset of winter.

The best time to pair birds is when they are in peak breeding condition. The birds should be bright and active and look as if they are raring to go—hens bounce from perch to perch and very often crouch on the perch and at the same time flap their wings vigorously. Their beak will have turned almost black by this time. The cocks become very active and sometimes go through the routine of vigorous flapping of wings. Cocks in breeding condition spend a lot of time singing and their beaks change to a pearly white.

Left: A pair of Red-headed Normal Gouldian Finches displaying the characteristic bill colours associated with good breeding condition. The hen (right) displays less red on the head and has a darker beak.
Below: The selection of healthy, alert birds is vital to a successful breeding program.

Selecting Stock

You should only purchase high quality healthy individuals from a reputable breeder who keeps detailed breeding and identification records. Before you buy, enquire about prices and inspect the stock of a number of aviculturists. The more birds you observe the better equipped you will be to select healthy birds. If necessary place the bird in a box for closer observation.

A healthy bird should exhibit the following:

- The bird should be of good size and type.
- The bird should be active and show no sign of lethargy.
- Eyes should be clear and alert.
- Feathering should be tight and have a healthy lustre. (Do not purchase birds during a moult.)
- Pin-tail feathers should be long.
- The vent should be clean and dry.
- Feet and legs should be clean, smooth and shiny.
- Flight should be swift.

Other points to consider when purchasing your birds:

- Enquire about the parentage of the birds and fertility rates. Maintain your collection with as wide a genetic base as possible.
- Observe the environment in which the birds are housed including access to sunlight, the weather and temperature conditions.

Yellow-headed Gouldian Finch cock.

- Try to obtain stock from an area with similar weather conditions to your own.
- Enquire about their diet, including protein and greenfood sources.
- Purchase juveniles. They have a longer life span. Most finches are past their best at four years of age.
- Purchase and transport your birds home in the morning to allow adequate time for the birds to settle into their new environment—in quarantine.

If you buy birds sight unseen, seek a guarantee from the breeder that unsuitable birds can be returned within a mutually agreed timeframe.

Black-headed Normal Gouldian Finch cock.

Establishing Breeding Pairs

There are a variety of ways of pairing your birds prior to the commencement of the breeding season. Some aviculturists prefer to allow the birds to select their own mates. The reduced aggression and increased harmony amongst pairs will improve breeding success. Other aviculturists use line-breeding techniques, usually to improve a specific aspect of the bird, such as type, colour or even fertility. These methods have advantages and disadvantages, so we leave it to the reader to assess what method suits their purposes best.

Fertility is paramount to future breeding success. The selection of pairs is the single most important ingredient for determining offspring quality and establishing a family of healthy Gouldians. Fertility is known to be a hereditary characteristic passed down the cock line. Ron Tristram uses an 'Alfa male/female system' that employs the same selection processes found in nature to improve fertility and production. He places three or four pairs of young birds from a strong genetic and fertility background into flights measuring approximately 3.5 metres long x 1 metre wide x 3 metres high to select their own partners.

He believes that pair bonding (ie allowing the birds to select their own mates) creates better breeding results and warns that extreme vigilance during this process is necessary as fighting for partners may lead to death. The fact that these birds determine their own mate and nesting sites results in them becoming prolific producers of high quality stock.

He likes and encourages Alfa birds, believing that this is the law of the wild. Both hens and cocks can become aggressive. This aggression is a sign of virility but great care must be taken to avoid deaths during the pairing process. Overly aggressive pairs should be immediately moved to single pair housing where they are able to concentrate on their breeding activities (Tristram pers. comm.).

Continuing good health

Pair of Yellow-headed Gouldian Finches.

and breeding relies upon starting with known proven stock and culling any weak breeders. Once a proven and healthy family of Gouldians has been acquired, further improvements should be continuously explored. Not every bird bred, even from a very good producing family will become a good breeder. Improvements to breeding ability are achieved by continually assessing the breeding results of every pair and the vitality of their young. Good record keeping will help identify the level of production of each pair and is therefore the starting point and key to creating a lasting and strong family of Gouldians.

The number of young produced by each pair of Gouldians over a breeding season is known as fecundity. Although fecundity is the best measure of the genetic breeding performance of a pair (this quality being passed on to offspring), there are other more immediate signs that can be used to select the best quality breeders. Assertive cocks, juveniles that moult rapidly and individual birds that remain in good physical condition (active, tight-feathered and with an upright stance) under adverse weather conditions are important signs of virility and these should be the first birds chosen as breeders.

The process for improving the strength of the Gouldian family is a continual one and relies principally upon the selection of the best breeding pairs to replace lesser breeders. A healthy family with a strong genetic background of breeding success is required before improvements to a family can be made. Although breeding ability is a strong heritable characteristic passed down from generation to generation, there still remains a high degree of variation in the breeding ability of the offspring. For this reason, selection is a process that must be continually tested for every pair on an individual nest basis.

Ron Tristram (pers. comm.) maintains that it is extremely important when developing a strain or type of Gouldian Finch to be aware of each variety's strengths and weaknesses. Weaknesses must be strengthened by way of biodiversity (ie introducing new strong bloodlines).

Line Breeding

The practice of line breeding is an age-old method where related individuals are paired in order to maintain and improve certain characteristics such as colour or body shape. Although talked about often it is probably fair to suggest that very few breeders actually put into practice the true theory of line breeding.

It is worth remembering that line breeding has many pitfalls to trap both the novice and experienced breeder. Line breeding, although vehemently refuted by enthusiasts, is basically a form of inbreeding. In many instances the aim of producing better birds by pairing individuals that are closely related not only has the effect of doubling the 'good genes', it also has the effect of doing the same with unwanted genes. These 'bad genes' can lurk as recessive characteristics that only appear when both the parents are carriers.

A spectacular collection of Black-headed Normal Gouldian Finches.

In birds this is often revealed in a phenotype with the appearance of poorly positioned wings or unwanted blemishes in the plumage. If you are to embark on a line-breeding program, ensure that only the best available birds are used and check the parents, grandparents and any other related birds whenever possible.

It is often suggested that a line-breeding program begin with unrelated birds. This method tends to reduce the likelihood of both parents having unwanted hidden traits that immediately become a problem at the start. More advanced systems also employ a method where several different lines are kept simultaneously. This proves quite valuable later in the breeding program because eventually there will be a need for an 'outcross'—an unrelated bird. It is more convenient if you already own the outcross and know its genetic background. With outcrosses you always run the risk of introducing more unwanted recessive traits.

1. Yellow-headed White-breasted SF Pastel Green Gouldian Finch.
2. Red-headed White-breasted DF Pastel Green cock.
3. Yellow-headed Dilute-backed Gouldian Finch cock.
4. Red-headed Blue Gouldian Finch cocks.
5. Red-headed Dilute-backed Gouldian Finch hen.

After the first breeding season the parents are kept and mated back to their parents. Basically the systems works by selecting the best young from each generation and re-pairing these young back to the original birds from the first year. The system is followed for four generations by pairing father to daughter, grandfather to granddaughter, great-grandfather to great-granddaughter and great-great-grandfather to great-great-granddaughter. After four generations the young are genetically almost identical—not necessarily phenotypically—to the original parent that they were re-paired with throughout the process. This system can be used for both the original birds, creating two lines that at the end of four generations can again be re-paired to start again. However the process should be reviewed following each breeding season and, if there are problems, the situation should be reassessed. A useful review of this system is given in Leaney and Williams (1993).

Black-headed White-breasted Green Gouldian Finch.

Incompatibility

Failure to breed is mostly due to incompatibility, assuming of course that the birds are in good breeding condition. A bird that is not one hundred percent healthy will not attain breeding condition. Incompatibility is not a problem when colony breeding because birds will choose their own partners. If, on the other hand, your birds are housed as individual pairs in separate aviaries or cages you must watch closely for signs of incompatibility.

The cock always shows his keenness to pair by displaying to the hen soon after being introduced. If, a few days after introduction, the birds start showing signs of aggression by beak fencing, perching apart and showing complete disinterest in each other, then it is time to separate them and try them with other mates.

Red-headed Normal Gouldian Finch cock in courtship display.

Courtship Behaviour

The courtship performance, which generally takes place on a perch or a horizontal branch, consists of two phases. In the first phase the cock perches obliquely. The face and head feathers are fluffed while at the same time the breast and abdomen feathers are also fluffed making the purple breast patch look bigger. Showing these brilliant colours to the hen is not enough to attract her attention. The cock must 'display' to the hen and this is done by first making a series of head movements in which the beak is wiped across the perch sometimes without touching it. This is followed by shaking his head to and fro extremely rapidly in front of the hen.

Suddenly the cock enters the second phase of his display. He adopts an upright stance on the perch and with his beak pointing downwards he starts bobbing up and down on the perch in a rigid stance as he sings his courtship song to the hen. This display is repeated several times during the courtship period. If the hen is receptive she will remain near him and will respond by twisting her tail towards him. If on the other hand she is unimpressed she will then fly away. Successful copulation usually takes place inside the nestbox. Many a time a cock tries to mate on a perch without success. The hen often rejects him instantly.

Interestingly we are now aware that many of the postures that the Gouldian Finch cock assumes during courtship have evolved to enhance the quality of his plumage with respect to how it is viewed by the hen. Many birds, including Gouldian Finches see within the UV wavelengths of light, an attribute humans do not possess. Aviculturists, therefore, are missing many of the signals that birds are giving. Recently experimental evidence (Lewis, unpublished data) has shown that the light source within a Gouldian Finch enclosure can determine the acceptability of prospective mates. If the lights used are incorrect in wavelength, ie they do not contain UV wavelengths, the hen does not obtain the correct breeding cues from the cock. This may partially explain why breeding success for Gouldian Finches housed indoors without access to natural light has been poor.

Nest Preparation

Offer the birds a choice of nestboxes, by providing a greater number of nestboxes than there are pairs of birds. As a general rule, it is preferable to supply twice the number of nestboxes as there are pairs. Hang them in different areas of the aviary, away from water and feed containers to prevent faeces or nestlings dropping into seed and water. When placing more than one pair in your breeding enclosure, you may see some aggression. This only occurs for a short time as parents protect the nest site.

Each nest has a preformed nest chamber of fine nesting material such as Couch, November Grass or similar. Some pairs are poor nest builders while others build very elaborate nests finishing off with a canopy. Nesting material should be supplied in liberal quantities in lengths of about 10–15cm in wire baskets located away from perches to avoid contamination from droppings. Alternatively, the nesting material could be placed in a corner on the aviary floor where some birds seem to prefer it. A few minutes after the nestbox has been put in place the cock will peer inside from the top of the box without entering it. The hen, who is never far from the cock, may sometimes inspect the nestbox soon after. The cock selects all the nesting material and builds the nest while the hen watches. When the cock has finished building the nest the hen enters the nestbox and as egg laying time approaches the pair spend more time together in the nestbox.

The cock carries all the nesting material and builds the nest.

A partial nest construction from lengths of grass.

An ideal nesting material is a combination of fine and coarse textured grasses.

November Grass has a fine texture.

Rolly Polly Grass has a coarse texture.

Charcoal in the bottom of the nestbox helps absorb moisture.

Egg Laying and Incubation

Within 10–15 days, sometimes longer, depending on the stage of breeding condition of the pair, the hen starts laying. She produces one white egg every day, which is generally laid in the morning. Clutches vary in size from 4–7 eggs, sometimes more. After the laying of the third egg the pair invariably, although not always, start incubating. Some pairs do not start sitting in earnest until the last egg is laid. Incubation is shared during the day while at night the hen incubates on her own. When actively incubating during the breeding season the cock and the hen develop a bare patch of skin on the abdomen. This brooding patch allows better heat transfer to the eggs. On day five of incubation fertile eggs become pinkish in colour, and if placed over a light source, blood veins are visible indicating that the embryo is developing. As the embryo grows the egg becomes chalky in colour. Hatching usually commences on days 15–16. Discarded eggshells are eaten by the parents, although at odd times one might see half a shell on the floor underneath the nestbox.

Nest of Gouldian Finch eggs.

Nestlings

The chicks are fed by both parents. The crop of a newly hatched chick extends to both sides of the neck, but only the right side is filled with food for the first few days. As the chick grows both sides are filled. Their begging calls for food are loud and can be heard several metres away. Newly hatched Gouldian Finch chicks are bare skinned (having no down) and are a light flesh colour. Their eyes open on day seven and the dark primary feathers break through the skin on days 11–12.

Softfood mixed with sprouted seed is supplied twice a day, morning and late afternoon. As the chicks grow so does their requirement for softfood and sprouted seed. Ensure that the parents have as much as they need at all times. All softfood containers are removed from the aviary before nightfall. This will ensure that no stale softfood is fed to the chicks first thing in the morning.

We recommend that the chicks be checked at

Above: Nestlings crammed with food.
Above left: Nestlings at 1–2 days of age.
Left: Normal Gouldian Finch chicks. Note the dark skin markings and dark feathers, which develop at approximately 5–6 days of age.

least once daily, assuming that the parents do not strongly object. Fortunately Gouldians do not normally object to nest inspections. These should be carried out in midafternoon. The inspection is necessary to check the condition of the chicks, that their crops are full and that their skin is smooth and shiny. Chicks' droppings also tell a story. Their droppings should be firm, black or yellow in part (depending on the type of softfood supplied) and the remainder white.

Nestlings on the Floor

Some Gouldian Finches are known to remove their young from the nest and drop them onto the floor which results in the death of the young. It is difficult to understand the cause for this behaviour. However a number of reasons are regularly put forward. Some breeders maintain that the birds are seeking to put predators such as lizards off the scent of the main nest or that the parent birds are not in good enough condition to complete the breeding cycle. Some suggest aviary intrusion as the problem while others maintain that the young are deformed or weak. This appears to be a problem associated specifically with Gouldian Finches and has existed for many years.

One solution which appears to be successful in many cases has been to change the shape of the nestbox to prevent young falling out. This can be achieved by tilting the nestbox, extending its length or providing a double entrance to the nest. These solutions all appear to have merit which would lend support to the theory that disturbances to the adults, followed by a rapid departure from the nest, have caused the loss of nestlings.

Fledglings

Juvenile Gouldian Finches. Note the characteristic blue bill nodules.

Chicks fledge on days 24–26. They rarely return to their nest to roost. Instead they huddle together on a branch or perch, often flanked by their parents. They become self-sufficient 12–15 days after fledging. At about this time the parents are beginning to prepare for their next brood so the chicks should be removed and placed in holding cages and remain there until the end of the breeding season. When the breeding season is over the nesting receptacles are removed and all the youngsters are transferred to aviaries to moult and colour up.

Moult

The moult season will vary according to the geographical location and housing situation. The appearance of feathers on the cage or aviary floor indicates the beginning of moult. When pin-feathers develop on the head it indicates the onset of the breeding season.

Juvenile birds start moulting at 6–8 weeks of age. The process is a rather slow one taking some months. The juvenile Gouldian plumage is replaced in a progressive manner gradually revealing the adult colours. The feathers of the abdomen are the first to be replaced followed by those in the rump area. The breast patch begins to moult at about

Juvenile midway through a moult.

Gouldian Finch during a moult.

the same time as the head. The feathers on the back and wings are the last to be renewed followed by the pin-feathers.

Youngsters complete their juvenile moult at the same time as adults. Youngsters bred from February–August will retain their juvenile plumage until spring when the moult should occur. Birds that fledge late (July/August) should also moult during spring, attaining adult plumage around December (in the Southern Hemisphere). However, some birds bred late in the season will not always moult completely and they become 'stuck-in-the-moult' for the remainder of the year. These birds will moult successfully the following season.

It does not always follow that birds which do not moult completely were bred late in the season. A health setback, eg a bacterial infection due to overcrowding or lack of hygiene, could also cause a bird to get 'stuck-in-the-moult'.

Adult birds start moulting when the breeding season finishes. Shedding one coat of feathers and growing a new one poses an enormous drain on the birds' resources. This is a particularly stressful time and their resistance to bacterial infection is very low. Everything possible must be done to reduce stress and housing the birds in overcrowded conditions at this time will only produce more stress. Hygiene is very important at all times but more so during the moult. Soiled floors, aviary walls and perches all harbour bacteria, and should be cleaned regularly using Aviclens™, Halamid™ or a similar product. Food and water containers should be clean at all times and situated away from perches.

Some breeders experience juvenile losses during the moult. This could be due to an incorrect diet. It is said that feathers consist of approximately 90% protein. A diet rich in protein, eg egg food, sprouted seeds or softfoods, should be supplied daily to the birds until the moult is complete. (See *Moult Diet* page 41.)

Losses will be greatly minimised if you avoid overcrowding the birds, maintain a high level of hygiene and supply the correct diet.

Foster-parenting

There are three ways of rearing Gouldian Finches: parent rearing, fostering by Bengalese Finches and fostering by other Gouldian Finches.

Gouldian Finches are likely to be less successful as parents when they are diseased or weakened from poor housing, feeding, hygiene or genes. Strong families of Gouldian Finches make exceptional parents capable of rearing a clutch of as many as nine young. Blue mutations are often poorer parents and often foster-parents are required to rear their young and establish a family.

Bengalese Finches as Foster-parents

The subject of fostering using Bengalese Finches is open to debate and often argued. However, there appear to be some disadvantages in using Bengalese Finches as foster-parents.

One disadvantage is the possibility of imprinting. Gouldian Finches raised by

Bengalese Finches may learn the behaviours of their foster-parents. Some breeders suggest that imprinted birds will often not complete incubation. Yet other breeders have found that some of their best Gouldian Finch parents have been individuals raised by Bengalese Finch foster-parents. Evidence of negative imprinting has been observed in other species such as Zebra Finches raised by Bengalese Finches. However little research has been done with Gouldian Finches. It is highly possible that some behavioural traits such as courtship behaviour, song and perhaps even preferences for colour pattern are passed on by Bengalese Finch foster-parents to young Gouldian Finches. However, at this point in time, it appears that fostered Gouldian Finches breed successfully with Gouldian Finches raised by their natural parents.

Imprinting is of less concern than the increased likelihood of contracting a disease from the parents of a different species. The Gouldian Finch is highly susceptible to Thrush (*Candida*) infections which can be carried unnoticed by Bengalese Finches—a valid reason for concern. Although Bengalese Finches have often been thought to assist in preventing Air Sac Mite infestations in Gouldian Finches, they may however, carry infections—*Campylobacter, Cochlosoma* and Thrush (*Candida*)—that kill nestling and juvenile birds. Medicines have been required to control these diseases in young mutations reared by foster-parents. These medicines have further hampered the development of these weak families. It has also been suggested that Bengalese Finches are used as foster-parents purely for financial gain rather than for the long-term benefit of the Gouldian Finch.

Young Gouldian Finches with their Bengalese foster-mother.

Everything can be taken to extreme and with this in mind the reader is directed to several paragraphs from Ziegler (1975). Here the methodology of producing Gouldian Finches in large numbers in Japan was described in some detail. Apparently by using pairs of Bengalese Finches at least two broods of Gouldian Finches per season could be raised by each foster pair. At about eight months of age the Gouldian Finches were exported to the USA and Europe however, the mortality rate was very high. The young Gouldian Finches were described as having become 'implanted on the fosters' and as a result had lost their own natural instinct to breed with their own species.

It was also revealed that the Japanese breeder was able to take as many as 60 eggs from one Gouldian Finch hen. The ethics of this practice would now be questioned, being somewhat akin to battery farming and egg production in commercial chickens. However, this action was probably only practised by a few individuals with purely financial motives. In this case it is not fostering that is the problem, it is the suffering of the hens that is questioned. It appears that the practice was short-lived as most 'bad' practices are and the market soon fell away because of poor quality stock.

Some breeders suggest one advantage. The establishment of several mutations has been more rapid and may not have even occurred without fostering. Nowadays, the use of Bengalese Finches as foster-parents should be reserved for mutations that are poor parents or used to establish a new colour mutation. However, the problems associated with imprinting and the spread of illness make the argument for using Bengalese Finches as foster-parents less appealing.

Gouldian Finches as Foster-parents

The use of other Gouldian Finches, eg Normals with a good parenting background, as foster-parents is perhaps more acceptable to some aviculturists as it avoids any problem of imprinting with another species. It also negates the problem of introducing hidden diseases carried by a species that is more disease resistant. The eggs are simply exchanged between Normal and mutation pairs. The weaker mutation parents are given stronger Normal chicks to rear. This enhances parenting skills and improves the likelihood of the pair successfully rearing the clutch. The stronger, Normal pairs with proven parenting skills provide the weaker coloured mutation chicks with the best possible conditions to develop into strong and robust birds, offering them a better opportunity to breed successfully as adults. Over time, this system promotes a stronger family of Normal and coloured birds capable of breeding naturally.

Some breeders began using Gouldian Finches as foster-parents as a temporary measure to ensure the survival and continued breeding of less hardy mutations. It has been trialled with Blue series birds that were laying but not sitting on their eggs. Therefore fostering was seen as the best option. Three pairs of foster-parent birds produced the following results: 48 eggs were fostered, nine young fledged, eight young died in the nest, three nests were deserted, 28 eggs were fertile and 20 eggs were infertile. The quality of the young birds produced appeared to be excellent and the body size was acceptable and could only improve. It is important to note in this case that the parents were less than one year of age and naïve, which probably limited their success. Clearly this method can be successful and if used sensibly offers another option for those breeders not wishing to use Bengalese Finches as foster-parents.

Fostering Method

If you choose to foster using Bengalese Finches, they should be housed on their own. It is suggested that at least three pairs of Bengalese Finches be kept for each breeding pair of Gouldian Finches. You are then assured of having enough Bengalese Finches in the same nesting cycle when the Gouldians start laying. This is a very time-consuming venture and not necessarily always successful. For the most part Bengalese Finches are very good

Bengalese Finches are an option for foster-parenting. There are disadvantages to be considered if using this species as foster-parents.

parents. However, this is not always the case and some losses of young Gouldian Finches can occur. It is, therefore, very important to select quality Bengalese Finches bred in cages (not aviaries) for the specific purpose of foster-parenting.

The most successful aviculturists in this field have systematically selected Gouldian or Bengalese Finches from successive generations to produce excellent lines of foster-parents. This avoids having to start from scratch with birds of unknown fostering ability.

To begin the process it is usually necessary to house the Gouldian or Bengalese Finch pairs in breeding conditions similar to those used for canaries or well-domesticated finches such as the Zebra Finch (Lewis et al 2000). These finches can also be housed as single pairs in small wire cages stacked three or four cages high. This very successful system, commonly used in Europe, is both highly efficient and hygienic. Cages measuring 45cm long x 30cm deep x 35cm high should be used. These cages are made of 25mm x 12.5mm mesh, using special clips and pliers to fix the sides to the roof and base. The front of the cage should have all the required openings to enable the cage to be serviced from the outside. Opening allowances should be made for a breeding box, seed and water container, softfood container and an opening for access into the cage for catching birds when required. A metal tray is made for the bottom of the cage. The purpose of this tray is to make cage cleaning easier. It slides in and out through a slot made in the front. Some breeders use a box-type cage with a wire front. The advantage of this design is that disease cannot be transmitted from one cage to another. The same effect could be achieved by placing wire cages 10cm apart. One great advantage with the wire cage is hygiene. At the end of the breeding season it is taken out of the breeding room and completely immersed in a tub in a solution of water and disinfectant.

The door and nestbox opening can be made of the same 25mm x 12.5mm mesh. The wire door of course, is made larger than the opening it is required to cover. The door is hinged while the nestbox door is hooked onto the opening when the nestbox is not in use. The cages are placed against a wall in rows three or four high.

To begin the fostering process simply put your foster-parent and Gouldian Finch pairs to nest and wait for eggs. When the Gouldian Finches are laying, a choice needs to be made. Do you remove the eggs as they are produced or wait until the clutch is complete? A good reason for waiting and giving the foster-parents the entire clutch to incubate is that all the young should then hatch on the same day. In theory young that hatch on the same day grow at the same rate and fledge at about the same time. Therefore there is less likelihood of having nests with smaller weaker, siblings that sometimes die because of competition from larger siblings. If this system is chosen, the eggs should be removed each day, stored in a cool place and turned daily to prevent the embryo from adhering to the wall of the shell.

Alternatively the eggs can be left with the Gouldian Finch parents until the egg laying is finished, and then carefully removed and placed with the Gouldian or Bengalese Finch foster-parents that should also be at the incubating stage. Unfortunately at this point the foster-parent eggs must also be removed and either fostered under other finches or discarded. It would be unwise to increase the competition for food by leaving nestlings together as it will only lead to poor results. After the young leave the nest and are feeding independently, they should be removed to allow the foster-parents time to recover. If using Bengalese Finches it is also recommended that a spare adult Gouldian Finch be placed with the fledglings. This appears to help in the process of accepting both new housing and new foods in the coming months. In most cases it is a simple matter of retaining a few spare Gouldian Finch cocks for this purpose.

Record Keeping

The Gouldian Finch needs a broad genetic base if healthy stocks are to be maintained. To assist this need we must keep records of individual pairings as well as leg rings to record nestlings from each individual pair. The use of leg rings enables the keeper to identify the birds in order to select and pair them for the following season. Closed rings can be purchased from finch clubs. Split plastic rings can be purchased from pet stores or directly from manufacturers. Closed rings are placed on the legs of young while still in the nest at about 10 days of age. Split plastic rings can be placed on birds of any age.

There are also a variety of very good database computer programs that allow storage of large amounts of information. This data/information can be easily retrieved and viewed as parental lineages. It is even possible to compile graphs of aspects about the breeding season such as nest success.

Breeding Mutations—Considerations

Gouldian Finches bred in captivity may be separated into two groups—Normals and mutations. The housing and care of each group vary according to their breeding capacity and ability to stay alive in captivity. Normals are strong, prolific breeders whereas some mutations are weak and are often unable to rear their young successfully. The ability of each group varies from family to family and from strain to strain. The common goal of Gouldian Finch enthusiasts is to strengthen the families they keep and produce birds that breed prolifically, rear their own young and remain fit and healthy under the conditions in which they live.

The challenge of breeding mutations is met by paying attention to their specialised feeding and housing requirements. The selection of strong and vital individuals as breeders will also ensure the long-term viability of the family. Some mutations have been established for several years and with patience and wise breeding strategies have become hardy birds, good breeders and capable of rearing their own young.

Some mutations are as strong as Normals. However, some mutations, notably the Blue series mutations, may be extremely weak and require extraordinary levels of care and dedication. Blue mutations are particularly susceptible to Thrush (*Candida*), Coccidiosis, *Streptococcus, Campylobacter* and *Cochlosoma* infections. This mutation is not usually kept in a normal aviary environment. Large numbers of Blue mutations have been irreversibly imprinted on Bengalese Finches and need to be fostered with other Gouldian Finches instead if the imprinting issue is to be addressed and rectified (Tristram, pers. comm.).

Some mutations are poor parents and foster-parents are required to rear their young. In addition, artificial heating, cage breeding and medical aid are often the only way to establish the weaker families of popular mutations.

Mutations are more likely to die in the nest, at fledging, during adolescence, during the moult and upon exposure to disease. However, when established and wherever possible, mutations should be housed outdoors where they can receive the benefits of natural sunlight, fresh air and free flight. It is the improved fitness levels and associated health levels achieved through the conditions that exist in outdoor aviaries that produce a more naturally vital and potent family of Gouldian Finches. It is almost impossible to achieve a strong family of mutations without the benefits offered by outdoor aviaries.

Although many mutations have been established or are under development the breeding of Normal birds must continue. Overseas breeders cannot import Normal Gouldians from Australia. In their native country wild populations are declining. The fate of these birds could now rest in the hands of aviculturists. Mutations have their place but not at the expense of the Normal bird. It could well be that in the future the Normal Gouldian Finch will be more sought after than any mutation. However, before that situation arises we should ensure the safety of these truly magnificent finches.

Above: Black-headed SF Pastel Blue Gouldian Finch hen.

Right: Yellow-headed White-breasted DF Pastel Gouldian Finch cock.

Left: Yellow-headed White-breasted Green Gouldian Finch cock.

Below: Yellowtip Bill Black-headed White-breasted Green Gouldian Finch hen.

Health Difficulties in Mutations

The unenviable challenge for some Gouldian enthusiasts is to produce healthy coloured mutations in large numbers. This is no easy task as unknown genetic flaws that weaken offspring lurk in the aberrant mutations. Inbreeding is essential for creating a coloured strain, but this often produces weak, 'coloured' offspring, complicating the development of a viable healthy strain even further.

Gouldian Finch mutations generally require more precise care than Normals throughout their entire life cycle but especially prior to the start of breeding. The preparations for breeding are more complicated for mutations. Kept under less spacious indoor conditions, mutations do not receive the same health and fitness benefits as Normal Gouldian Finches.

It is difficult to explain exactly why mutations are less hardy than Normals. In the wild the selection process is continual and an entrenched feature for maintaining the strength and future of all species, not only the Gouldian Finch. Current understanding by behavioural scientists confirms that hens select those cocks that display the greatest vigour under the negative physiological circumstances of testosterone release. Fox *et al* (2002) recognised that during the breeding season hens were attracted to cocks with certain physical features, such as an increased length of tail pin-feather and a larger bill size. These characteristics of the Gouldian Finch probably represent attributes that enhance survivorship or parental abilities. They have been an evolutionary development in the wild with a prime objective of ensuring that the best genes are made available to future generations. Even so, the progeny from the 'strongest' pairs are not always vital and strong because genetic variation from one offspring to the next always occurs. Genetic variation produces both weaklings and the diversity necessary for evolutionary change—the basis of future success for all species.

Problems associated with mutations originate from inherent weaknesses. Chances of producing weak offspring are greater than when breeding from strong individuals or pairs. Protection from fluctuating environmental conditions, addition of nutritional supplements, programs for disease prevention and careful selection of each breeding pair help to produce strong lineages of mutations. For example, the chances of producing strong Blue offspring are improved when Blue mutations are paired with hardy and healthy split Blue mutations.

MUTATIONS AND COLOUR BREEDING

*Yellow-headed
White-breasted SF
Pastel Gouldian
Finch hen*

D VAN DEN ABEELE

Red-headed Normal Gouldian Finch cock.

Black-headed Normal cock.

Yellow-headed Normal hen.

Breeding Head Colours

There are three basic head colours in the Gouldian Finch—Red-headed, Black-headed and Yellow-headed. Ideally the head colours should not be bred together indiscriminately. By doing so a number of motley blackish red or blackish yellow-headed birds are produced. This is especially prevalent in hens. When selecting for head-colour breeding, special attention should be paid to the hens used for breeding. Black-headed hens especially should be a rich deep velvety black with absolutely no signs of a red or yellow feather showing through.

Pairing different head colours should only be done for a particular reason, eg to improve the quality of the finch itself. If all the Yellow-headed birds in the aviary are of poor quality, ie too small or have poor fertility, then they should be mated through your other head colours to rectify these deficiencies. Buying good quality Yellow-headed stock may seem a better solution but remember that many problems can be brought into your established stock by new arrivals. Only use newly acquired birds when absolutely necessary, making sure that you follow appropriate quarantine measures or disaster will most certainly follow. You may also wish to breed a mutation in the three head colours. If, for example, all your Dilute-backed Gouldians are Black-headed, then to produce Red-headed Dilutes they have to be paired to Red-headed birds.

The Red-headed is sex-linked dominant and has a red-tipped beak. The Black-headed is sex-linked recessive and can have a red-tipped or a yellow-tipped beak. The Normal Black-headed Gouldian has a red-tipped beak. The Yellow-headed is autosomal recessive and has a yellow-tipped beak. When a Gouldian Finch inherits both the characteristics for black and yellow-headedness the black will mask the yellow. That is to say, it is a Yellow-headed bird with a black head and not simply a Black-headed bird split to Yellow-headed. Therefore because it is Yellow-headed it has a yellow-tipped beak. A Black-headed Gouldian split to Yellow-headed will have a red-tipped beak.

Mating Expectations

Breeders often become either confused or frustrated over tables of mating expectations. Perhaps because the word 'expectation' is used, people think that they should always expect to produce all the coloured young in the 'expected' percentages. The truth is that these are tables of 'odds'. They incorporate statistics and chance to give an indication of what colours and genetic make-ups might be produced and in what proportions.

Only colours and make-ups listed in an expectation table can be produced from a particular mating. And the proportions give us an idea of the likelihood of breeding each of the possibilities. However just like a horserace, the short-priced favourite may not win and a long shot may sneak through. (Although if they are not in the race they cannot win!)

The way to use tables of mating expectations is to first determine what you might produce from a mating, to ensure that your desired outcome is in there somewhere. Next, you can compare different matings to decide if a 'better' mating might be possible to produce a greater chance of a certain colour than another.

However in the end, the young produced will only approach the proportions given in the expectation tables when hundreds are produced. In the same way, the chance of tossing heads or tails on a coin is 50:50, yet you can still toss four heads in a row. However the chance of throwing 10 heads in a row is very low. Always keep in mind the value and purpose of mating expectations and do not expect more from them than they can give.

TABLE OF MATING EXPECTATIONS

PARENTS COCK X HEN	PROGENY	
	COCKS	HENS
Red x Red	50% Red	50% Red
Red x Black	50% Red split Black	50% Red
Red split Black x Red	25% Red 25% Red split Black	25% Red 25% Black
Red split Black x Black	25% Red split Black 25% Black	25% Red 25% Black
Red x Yellow	50% Red split Yellow	50% Red split Yellow
Red split Yellow x Red split Yellow	12.5% Red 25% Red split Yellow 12.5% Yellow	12.5% Red 25% Red split Yellow 12.5% Yellow
Red split Yellow x Yellow	25% Red split Yellow 25% Yellow	25% Red split Yellow 25% Yellow
Red split Yellow x Red	25% Red 25% Red split Yellow	25% Red 25% Red split Yellow
Red x Red split Yellow	25% Red 25% Red split Yellow	25% Red 25% Red split Yellow
Red split Black x Yellow	25% Red split Yellow 25% Red split Black split Yellow	25% Red split Yellow 25% Black split Yellow
Red split Black split Yellow x Black split Yellow	6.25% Red split Black 6.25% Black 12.5% Red split Black split Yellow 12.5% Black split Yellow 6.25% Yellow split Black 6.25% Black Yellowtip Bill	6.25% Red 6.25% Black 12.5% Red split Yellow 12.5% Black split Yellow 6.25% Yellow 6.25% Black Yellowtip Bill

TABLE OF MATING EXPECTATIONS (cont.)

PARENTS COCK X HEN	PROGENY	
	COCK	**HEN**
Red split Yellow x Black split Yellow	12.5% Red split Black 25% Red split Black split Yellow 12.5% Yellow split Black	12.5% Red 25% Red split Yellow 12.5% Yellow
Red x Black Yellowtip Bill	50% Red split Black split Yellow	50% Red split Yellow
Red split Yellow x Black Yellowtip Bill	25% Red split Black split Yellow 25% Yellow split Black	25% Red split Yellow 25% Yellow
Red split Black split Yellow x Black Yellowtip Bill	12.5% Red split Black split Yellow 12.5% Black split Yellow 12.5% Yellow split Black 12.5% Black Yellowtip Bill	12.5% Red split Yellow 12.5% Black split Yellow 12.5% Yellow 12.5% Black Yellowtip Bill
Red split Black x Black Yellowtip Bill	25% Red split Black split Yellow 25% Black split Yellow	25% Red split Yellow 25% Black split Yellow
Red split Black x Black split Yellow	12.5% Red split Black 12.5% Black 12.5% Red split Black split Yellow 12.5% Black split Yellow	12.5% Red 12.5% Black 12.5% Red split Yellow 12.5% Black split Yellow
Red x Black split Yellow	25% Red split Black 25% Red split Black split Yellow	25% Red 25% Red split Yellow
Red split Black split Yellow x Black	12.5% Red split Black 12.5% Black 12.5% Red split Black split Yellow 12.5% Black split Yellow	12.5% Red 12.5% Black 12.5% Red split Yellow 12.5% Black split Yellow
Red split Yellow x Black	25% Red split Black 25% Red split Black split Yellow	25% Red 25% Red split Yellow
Red split Black split Yellow x Red split Yellow	6.25% Red 6.25% Red split Black 12.5% Red split Yellow 12.5% Red split Black split Yellow 6.25% Yellow 6.25% Yellow split Black	6.25% Red 6.25% Black 12.5% Red split Yellow 12.5% Black split Yellow 6.25% Yellow 6.25% Black Yellowtip Bill
Red split Black split Yellow x Yellow	12.5% Red split Yellow 12.5% Red split Black split Yellow 12.5% Yellow 12.5% Yellow split Black	12.5% Red split Yellow 12.5% Black split Yellow 12.5% Yellow 12.5% Black Yellowtip Bill

TABLE OF MATING EXPECTATIONS (cont.)

PARENTS COCK X HEN	PROGENY COCK	HEN
Red split Black x Red split Yellow	12.5% Red 12.5% Red split Black 12.5% Red split Yellow 12.5% Red split Black split Yellow	12.5% Red 12.5% Black 12.5% Red split Yellow 12.5% Black split Yellow
Red split Black split Yellow x Red	12.5% Red 12.5% Red split Black 12.5% Red split Yellow 12.5% Red split Black split Yellow	12.5% Red 12.5% Black 12.5% Red split Yellow 12.5% Black split Yellow
Black x Black	50% Black	50% Black
Black x Red	50% Red split Black	50% Black
Black x Yellow	50% Red split Black split Yellow	50% Black split Yellow
Black x Red split Yellow	25% Red split Black 25% Red split Black split Yellow	25% Black 25% Black split Yellow
Black split Yellow x Red	25% Red split Black 25% Red split Black split Yellow	25% Black 25% Black split Yellow
Black split Yellow x Red split Yellow	12.5% Red split Black 25% Red split Black split Yellow 12.5% Yellow split Black	12.5% Black 25% Black split Yellow 12.5% Black Yellowtip Bill
Black split Yellow x Black split Yellow	12.5% Black 25% Black split Yellow 12.5% Black Yellowtip Bill	12.5% Black 25% Black split Yellow 12.5% Black Yellowtip Bill
Black split Yellow x Yellow	25% Red split Black split Yellow 25% Yellow split Black	25% Black split Yellow 25% Black Yellowtip Bill
Black x Black split Yellow	25% Black 25% Black split Yellow	25% Black 25% Black split Yellow
Black Yellowtip Bill x Black	50% Black split Yellow	50% Black split Yellow
Black x Black Yellowtip Bill	50% Black split Yellow	50% Black split Yellow
Black Yellowtip Bill x Black split Yellow	25% Black split Yellow 25% Black Yellowtip Bill	25% Black split Yellow 25% Black Yellowtip Bill
Black split Yellow x Black Yellowtip Bill	25% Black split Yellow 25% Black Yellowtip Bill	25% Black split Yellow 25% Black Yellowtip Bill

TABLE OF MATING EXPECTATIONS (cont.)

PARENTS COCK X HEN	PROGENY	
	COCK	HEN
Black Yellowtip Bill x Black Yellowtip Bill	50% Black Yellowtip Bill	50% Black Yellowtip Bill
Black Yellowtip Bill x Yellow	50% Yellow split Black	50% Black Yellowtip Bill
Black Yellowtip Bill x Red split Yellow	25% Red split Black split Yellow 25% Yellow split Black	25% Black split Yellow 25% Black Yellowtip Bill
Black Yellowtip Bill x Red	50% Red split Black split Yellow	50% Black split Yellow
Yellow x Yellow	50% Yellow	50% Yellow
Yellow x Black	50% Red split Black split Yellow	50% Red split Yellow
Yellow x Black split Yellow	25% Red split Black split Yellow 25% Yellow split Black	25% Red split Yellow 25% Yellow
Yellow split Black x Yellow	25% Yellow 25% Yellow split Black	25% Yellow 25% Black Yellowtip Bill
Yellow split Black x Black split Yellow	12.5% Red split Black split Yellow 12.5% Black split Yellow 12.5% Yellow split Black 12.5% Black Yellowtip Bill	12.5% Red split Yellow 12.5% Black split Yellow 12.5% Yellow 12.5% Black Yellowtip Bill
Yellow split Black x Black	25% Red split Black split Yellow 25% Black split Yellow	25% Red split Yellow 25% Black split Yellow
Yellow x Red	50% Red split Yellow	50% Red split Yellow
Yellow split Black x Red	25% Red split Yellow 25% Red split Black split Yellow	25% Red split Yellow 25% Black split Yellow
Yellow x Red split Yellow	25% Red split Yellow 25% Yellow	25% Red split Yellow 25% Yellow
Yellow split Black x Red split Yellow	12.5% Red split Yellow 12.5% Red split Black split Yellow 12.5% Yellow 12.5% Yellow split Black	12.5% Red split Yellow 12.5% Black split Yellow 12.5% Yellow 12.5% Black Yellowtip Bill
Yellow x Black Yellowtip Bill	50% Yellow split Black	50% Yellow
Yellow split Black x Black Yellowtip Bill	25% Yellow split Black 25% Black Yellowtip Bill	25% Yellow 25% Black Yellowtip Bill

MUTATIONS

Above: Black-headed Blue Gouldian Finch cock.
Right: Red-headed Blue Gouldian Finch cock.

Blue

All the green plumage in this bird is replaced by blue. The abdomen is creamy yellow to white. It can be easily distinguished from Dilute Blue because the Dilutes produce less melanin and they therefore lose the black bib and pencil lines around the face that the Blue retains. Black-headed Blue mutations can also be produced. Like all Blue mutations the mode of inheritance is autosomal recessive and can occur in all three breast colours—purple, lilac and white. In all of the Blue mutations so far the red or yellow beak-tip colours have been lost. In the nest Blue chicks have normal-coloured eyes but their skin appears to have a blue-grey haze.

Seagreen

This mutation has only been recently bred in Australia. Not a lot is known about it at present.

Sex-linked Pastel (Yellow-backed)

Overseas this bird is often referred to as the European Dilute. This will confuse many Australian Gouldian breeders because it is not the same as the recessive Dilute-backed. There is a strong move internationally to standardise the names of all mutations and Pastel has been chosen for this mutation to avoid confusion with other existing mutations.

The Pastel mutation is a co-dominant sex-linked mutation. At this stage it would be more beneficial to record for the

This Black-headed Seagreen Gouldian Finch hen shows that it is certainly different in colour from the other Blue mutations.

Left: Black-headed SF Pastel Gouldian Finch hen.
Below: Red-headed SF Pastel Gouldian Finch cock.

reader some of the things that happen with this mutation rather than why they happen.

All hens are Single Factor (SF). No Double Factor (DF) Pastel hens can be produced. The cock can be either Single Factor or Double Factor. As there can only be one phenotype (physical appearance) in the Double Factor Pastel cock, we will consider this bird first. This bird is similar in appearance to the Pastel hen but has the usual brighter purple chest of the cock. Overseas this bird was referred to as a 'European Yellow'. This again is confusing because it sounds like a separate mutation and you cannot get a pair of 'European Yellows' because only the cock can be a Double Factor. So here we shall refer to it as a Double Factor Pastel. Double Factor Pastel cocks occur in both purple and white-breasted forms.

The Single Factor Pastel cock does not resemble the Double Factor Pastel at all but looks more like a diluted version of a Normal Gouldian. This is another example of where a name can cause much confusion. In the USA it is not referred to as a Single Factor Pastel cock but as a 'Dilute'. Therefore when they refer to mating a 'Dilute' to a 'Yellow-backed' bird, they are simply mating a Single Factor Pastel cock to a Single Factor Pastel hen and not mating two different mutations. The Single Factor cock can be distinguished quite easily from the Normal Gouldian cock. Not simply because the green on the back is lighter or because the blue on the neck and rump is a softer shade but the Single Factor bird does not show the black markings of the Normal. The black bib, facial pencil lines, flights and tail feathers are all replaced by a fawny grey.

So far we have been talking about the Normal Purple-breasted Pastel in Single and Double Factor forms. When the White-breasted Gouldian is crossed with the Pastel more changes take place.

When White-breasted Pastel birds are produced their entire body becomes yellow. These birds look very much like the recessive Australian Yellows. The hen has much more yellow on the back than the cock. The cock shows the dilute effects typical of the Single Factor Pastel cock. He has a soft green wash through his back and the bib and neck markings are a grey-blue.

Yellow-headed DF Pastel Gouldian Finch cock.

Left: Red-headed SF Pastel Blue Gouldian Finch cock.

Below: Red-headed DF Pastel Blue Gouldian Finch cock.

When comparing the White-breasted and the Purple-breasted Pastel it is difficult to believe that differences have only been brought about by a change in breast colour. Overseas White-breasted Pastels are referred to as 'Yellow-bodied' Gouldians.

When the Blue Gouldian is bred through the Pastel bird the young produced in the first generation will include Pastel split Blue hens, Normal split Blue hens, Single Factor Pastel split Blue cocks and Normal split Blue cocks. It is in the second generation that we can expect to produce another colour from the Blue and Pastel genes. Here we find that the Blue series hens produced are either Blue or Single Factor Pastel Blue and the cocks produced are Single Factor Pastel Blue and Double Factor Pastel Blue (formerly known as Silver). It should be emphasised here that we are discussing Purple-breasted Blues and Pastel Blues. The Single Factor Pastel Blue cock is a beautiful bird of soft powdery blue colouring.

When the White-breasted mutation is paired with these birds, White-breasted Blue and White-breasted Pastel Blue hens, which are a lovely silver colour, are produced. In the cocks White-breasted Pastel Blues are a 'white-breasted silver' colour.

Hens will always be a silvery colour no matter whether they are Pastel Blue or White-breasted Pastel Blue, whereas Single Factor Pastel Blue cocks are light blue and Double Factor Pastel Blue, White-breasted Double Factor Pastel Blue or White-breasted Single Factor Pastel Blue birds are a silvery colour.

In Pastel mutations and their combinations only the Red-headed and Yellow-headed birds show normal colour. The Black-headed birds vary from a silver-grey to a creamy white.

It should be mentioned here that when breeding from certain Double Factor combinations a certain percentage of chicks produced will die in the nest. This is due to a lethal factor. It is unwise, therefore, to breed Double Factor cocks with Single Factor hens. Double Factor cocks should be bred with Normals or Blues to produce all Single Factor birds.

In the nest Pastel chicks have lighter eyes than the Normal at first but these darken again about seven days after opening. Their skin is more of a yellow-orange colour, very much like a jaundiced effect. The eyes of Pastel Blue ('Silver') chicks are also lighter to begin with but darken to that of the Normal. Their skin is a hazy silver-blue colour.

Briefly, we have discussed the following colours all stemming from the Pastel Gouldian: the Single Factor Pastel cock, the Double Factor Pastel cock, the Single Factor Pastel Blue cock and the Double Factor Pastel Blue cock.

Dilute-backed

This mutation first appeared in Queensland around 1945 and has to date still failed to become readily available. Over the past decade since the first edition of this book, the Dilute-backed has been confused with the sex-linked Pastel mutation from Europe. Many aviaries have held reasonable numbers of these birds at various times. Examples such as these and the loss of other mutations in the past indicate the real problems that many breeders were having with their Gouldians. Losses of Normals were no real problem in those days. Trapped birds made replacements easy to obtain. However, the Dilute-backed and other mutations were not obtainable in this fashion and so they died out or became scarce, not necessarily because they were weak birds but more probably because of poor management techniques.

Black-headed Dilute-backed Gouldian Finch cock.

The black throat or bib of the Normal is a creamy bluish white in the Dilute-backed, giving the Red-headed and Yellow-headed birds the appearance of wearing a bonnet. The back is a creamy lime-green colour. Because this mutation produces less melanin than normal the Black-headed bird has a silver-grey head.

In the nest Dilute-backed chicks have red eyes. However within a few days of their eyes opening, the eyes darken to that of the Normal. The skin is pink and the feathers are a creamy colour.

Australian Yellow

This very beautiful mutation is one of the most sought after in Australia. It is called the Australian Yellow to distinguish it from the White-breasted Sex-linked Pastel. Red-headed and Yellow-headed birds in this mutation can be produced but Black-headed birds have a white head devoid of all melanin.

In the nest young birds can be distinguished from Normals because they have white nodules on the sides of the beak as opposed to the blue nodules of the Normal Gouldian. When they leave the nest, young birds show variegated markings on their backs and bodies. The heaviness of these green, grey and white markings vary in amount from bird to bird. As they mature the most desirable birds lose these markings and develop a pure yellow back. Others retain the markings albeit usually to a lesser extent. A breeder reports that one youngster left the nest almost pure white only to moult into a lovely clear yellow. There is still much to be learnt about this mutation. Whether the variegated birds are a separate Pied mutation is still being debated.

Red-headed Australian Yellow hen (left) and Yellow-headed Australian Yellow cock.

Right: Yellowtip Bill Black-headed White-breasted Green Gouldian Finch hen.
Below: Yellow-headed White-breasted Green Gouldian Finch cock.
Below right: Red-headed White-breasted Green Gouldian Finch hen. (In the collection of Ray and Wendy Lowe.)

White-breasted

This mutation is identical to the Normal bird except that the purple breast is replaced by pure white. The White-breasted Gouldian can occur in all three head colours. It is recessive in its mode of inheritance.

Yellow-headed Lilac-breasted Green Gouldian Finch cock.

Lilac-breasted

This mutation which only differs from the Normal in breast colour, first appeared in the UK through breeding White-breasted and split White-breasted Gouldians. In the beginning the lilac appeared as small patches on the White-breasted bird and this was gradually improved. This is very interesting because in Australia these lilac patches are appearing on the breasts of some of our White-breasted mutations. One breeder here reports that a young Red-headed White-breasted Pastel cock showed these lilac patches and at two years of age was completely lilac. This bird still showed the white base feathers beneath the lilac front. This mutation is recessive to the Normal but dominant to the White-breasted.

The Lilac-breasted mutation should be treated with caution because it can easily spread through all your birds and pop up where it is unwanted. Purple-breasted birds are the most dangerous because they can carry the lilac factor without showing it visually. The simplest way to eradicate the lilac factor from your birds is to breed the White-breasted mutations. Select those birds with pure white breasts because lilac is dominant to the white breast and if they do not show lilac then they are not carrying it. If there is the slightest speck of lilac on the breast then it is carrying lilac. The lilac will increase over one to two years to ultimately cover the breast.

Weak Mutations

Much has been written and discussed regarding the 'weakness' of certain Gouldian Finch mutations, in particular the Blue mutation and its combinations. While the problems noted are real, it is important to remember that the cause of the trouble is seldom the mutated colour gene itself. Instead these problems of poor vigour and lack of disease resistance stem from breeding practices, in particular the inbreeding commonly employed to increase production of rare recessive genes.

Whenever we select for a mutation, keep in mind that dozens of other genes are linked to the one we are interested in and these 'passenger' genes have their own functions, which may become deleterious in some circumstances. If you consider that each new mutation appears because of a genetic error to a pre-existing wildtype gene, it might then be apparent that neighbouring genes might also be damaged at the same time. And while the colour mutant gene might not be harmful to the survival of the bird, some of these other genes might not be so benign.

Another problem arises through the use of inbreeding, which is always necessary in at least small degrees to produce birds exhibiting recessive traits. The function of inbreeding is to increase the chance of offspring carrying two identical versions of the desired gene. Unfortunately this same process acts upon the whole genetic make-up of the bird, reducing the degree of genetic variability within the individual. Without due care, the loss of genetic variability by the bird will result in reduced vitality and poor disease resistance.

Between these two processes, new mutations are often linked to unhealthy traits, which can be eliminated with time and careful breeding. The most important principle is to regularly outcross to different Normal lines—there is no point using just one family of Normals repeatedly as you will be inbreeding to those birds with the same adverse outcomes. Always keep this principle in mind when establishing a new mutation or if problems arise with the vigour of an established colour in your aviary.

RECESSIVE INHERITANCE TABLE

In the following table substitute the letter 'c' for the recessive mutation colour. Examples of recessive mutations are the Dilute-backed, the White-breasted, the Blue and the Australian Yellow.

MATING	PROGENY
NN x NN	100% NN
NN x cc	100% Nc
Nc x cc	50% Nc and 50% cc
NC x Nc	50% Nc and 25% NN and 25% cc
Nc x NN	50% Nc and 50% NN
cc x cc	100% cc

NN = A Normal bird
cc = A recessive coloured bird
Nc = A Normal split to a recessive colour

COLOUR MUTATIONS, GENETIC INHERITANCE AND GENE ACTION

From left to right: Red-headed, Black-headed and Yellow-headed colour morphs all exist in the wild population.

Which Head Colour is Wildtype?

The starting point for any investigation into the genetic inheritance and gene function of colour mutations in any species is to identify and recognise the wildtype colour morph as this is the base against which all colour changes are measured. It is also the reference point for all forms of inheritance. In some domesticated species with origins clouded in the mists of history (eg dogs or cattle), it can be difficult to determine which was the original colour of the wild animal. Fortunately, for most avicultural species this is relatively easy for we can still observe the animals in their natural state.

Red-headed Normal Gouldian Finch cock. This is the true wildtype colour. Black-headed and Yellow-headed colour morphs are mutations of this original colour.

However, the Gouldian Finch presents a unique difficulty as it has no less than three naturally occurring colour morphs in the wild. Which one should be viewed as the wildtype colour morph, the starting point from which all other colours vary? Tied in with recognising the correct wildtype, is the correct interpretation of gene function. If we consider simply the sex-linked locus that switches between Red-headed and Black-headed, does this locus control colour change from black into red or red into black?

For the past 30–40 years, it has been generally accepted within aviculture and also the scientific community that the Black-headed Gouldian Finch was the original wildtype colour morph. This has created much confusion about the function of the various genes and unnecessarily complicated the inheritance of the Yellow-headed mutation. Yet all this is based on a false premise—that the most common colour morph in the wild must be the wildtype.

The Red-headed Gouldian Finch is the true wildtype colour morph and was originally correctly recognised as such by Volker (1964). Subsequently, Brush and Seifried (1968) conducted further studies, identifying the different pigments found in Yellow-headed and Red-headed colour morphs as well as differences in feather structure between Red-headed and Black-headed morphs. Unfortunately they interpreted their research incorrectly and reversed the conclusions made by Volker. Until very recently, scientists have not given further study to the subject and aviculturists have universally believed that the Black-headed colour morph was the true wildtype.

There are a number of reasons why the Red-headed Gouldian Finch is the true wildtype; however the most irrefutable reason is really quite simple. The black pencil lines around the head of the Red-headed colour morph could not have evolved on a Black-headed bird where they are not visible. Decorative features on birds, like the pencil lines that outline the head region of the Gouldian Finch, serve to draw attention to particular areas of the plumage and are often significant features used in species recognition. Selection pressure through mate competition is the process by which they evolved and were refined. If the wildtype was Black-headed the pencil lines would not exist—they could not appear in the Red-headed colour morph through random chance.

Another important piece of evidence for the identity of the true wildtype was originally observed and reported by Brush and Seifried (1968) although it was misinterpreted at the time. The sex-linked locus, to which the Red-headed and Black-headed alleles belong, does not control the production of the red pigment canthaxanthin as is commonly reported. Instead the locus controls the structure of the head feathers, in particular their ability to carry and display canthaxanthin. The wildtype Red-headed colour morph has elaborate, specialised structure to carry the red pigment, while the mutant Black-headed colour morph has smaller feathers that lack this structure. The Black-headed colour morph still has the ability to produce canthaxanthin, as can be seen with the red bill tip.

Once we recognise and accept the Red-headed colour morph as the true wildtype, the Black-headed colour morph can be viewed simply as dysfunction of a feather structure gene and the genetics and the behaviour of all other mutations fall easily into place.

PIGMENTATION AND COLOUR PRODUCTION

A large part of gaining an understanding into the action of the colour mutations in the Gouldian Finch begins with understanding the distribution of pigments and structural elements within its plumage and how they interact together to produce the different colours we see. The Gouldian Finch is renowned for its bright gaudy colours and the distinct separation between them. Yet many of the same elements are present in more

Above: Red-headed Normal Gouldian Finch cock.
Right: Red-headed Normal Gouldian Finch hen.

Normal Green Budgerigar. Gouldian Finches produce green colours by the same process as Budgerigars.

than one region of the plumage and it is the differing combinations of elements that are able to produce the dramatically different colours.

If we look at the colours of finches as a family, most are various combinations of drab blacks, browns and greys, often with small areas of red or yellow pigment thrown into the mix. In contrast, the Gouldian Finch has bright structural green and purple in its plumage, colours more reminiscent of the parrot family. And in fact, the method used by the Gouldian to produce these colours is a kind of light distortion process identical to that used by parrots even though it has been evolved independently. Dr Richard Prum and coworkers (Prum *et al* 1999) have compared the structure of feathers from Gouldian Finches, Budgerigars and lovebirds and found that all three species distort light by the same process known as **constructive interference** and that the feathers are constructed in the same way.

The light effect is produced by a special structural feature within the medulla of the feather known as the cloudy layer. When a layer of black melanin pigment is present below the cloudy layer, light is distorted to produce blue wavelengths of light. If yellow pigment is added to the zone above (known as the cortex), the returning light waves appear green. Therefore green plumage is a combination of two different pigments (black and yellow) plus structural light distortion. The cloudy layer and its light distortion effect are also critical elements in the production of the purple breast colour.

Despite the similarities to parrots in their method and ability to produce colours in their feathers, there are distinct differences because Gouldians are still finches. And like all finches, Gouldian Finches are able to produce both major types of melanin—**eumelanin** and **phaeomelanin**—while parrots can only produce eumelanin. Eumelanin is the classic black melanin that we tend to think of immediately when we think of 'melanin'. It is responsible for producing black, brown and grey colours. It is also the melanin type that must be present in the centre of the feather to produce green and blue structural colours.

A Grey Zebra Finch cock. The chestnut-red cheekpatch of the Zebra Finch illustrates the colour of phaeomelanin.

The second melanin type, phaeomelanin, is the special element that parrots lack. This pigment is best visualised in the cheekpatch colour of the Zebra Finch: a rich chestnut-red colour, not true red and not brown, but something in between. However it is also present in smaller amounts throughout the plumage of most finches (Gouldian Finches included), often producing brownish or buff tones of colour. In Gouldian Finches it plays a very important and special role, replacing eumelanin in the medulla of breast feathers and therefore changing the light distortion frequency from blue into purple.

The fact that finch plumage has two different melanin pigments becomes important for understanding how various colour mutations work, as some mutations affect both pigments while others alter only the one melanin type.

Gouldian Finches have two other colours in their plumage, which are produced by a second class of pigments known as carotenoids. The base colour is a yellow pigment known as **lutein**, the second colour is a red pigment known as

Page 76

canthaxanthin. Some authors tend to treat these two pigments as completely separate entities; however it is important to realise that the yellow pigment shares gene control with the red pigments. If the bird is unable to deposit yellow colours, it will not be able to deposit red. It can, however, produce yellow without having red pigment in its plumage.

As mentioned already, different regions of the plumage carry different elements of colour production and hence appear as completely different colours. It is important, therefore, to discuss each plumage zone independently and for the reader to compare the differences in their mind. Please note that in the following sections I am only discussing the pigment distribution in the wildtype Gouldian Finch. The Red-headed colour morph is the true wildtype—the reasons why discussed in detail on page 74. Unless stated otherwise, information refers to the Normal Red-headed Gouldian Finch.

Red-headed Normal Gouldian Finch hen (left) and cock (below).

Head

The Gouldian Finch has three primary head colours, two of which are naturally occurring colour mutations and will be discussed in the mutation section. (See *Black-headed* page 79 and *Yellow-headed* page 80.)

The head region of the wildtype is predominantly red in colour, through the heavy deposition of canthaxanthin pigment in the extremities of the feathers. However there are also traces of melanin pigments present, both eumelanin (black) and phaeomelanin (chestnut), which become visible when the red pigment is removed by one of the colour mutations.

Under the throat is a **bib** of dense black due to heavy deposition of eumelanin in the outer areas of the feather. There are also small traces of phaeomelanin in this area as well. The black of the bib extends up around the head area in thin black markings known as **pencil lines**. These have the same pigment structure and composition as the throat area. The bill in cocks is horn-coloured, lacking melanin of either type (hens carry varying amounts of melanin), but has a small red marking on the tip comprised of canthaxanthin.

Neck

The neck of the Gouldian Finch cock has a blue collar following the outline of the black pencil lines. This is less developed in the hen. Blue colouration is produced through a combination of eumelanin (black pigment) deep within the medulla of the feather and overlaid by the special cloudy zone that creates the light distortion effect. This region lacks all carotenoid pigments, both yellow and red.

Back and Wings

The back and wings of the Gouldian Finch are green and comprise what would be referred to as the body colour of the bird. This is true green, not grey-green as we see in many other finch species like canaries and Star Finches. It is produced through the combined effects of three distinct components: yellow lutein pigment in the outer cortex of the feather, black eumelanin pigment deep in the medulla of the feather and the special structural cloudy layer lying immediately over the melanin. There are also traces of phaeomelanin in this region, although its presence is only detectable when other pigments are removed by some of the colour mutations. Like most species, the flight feathers are black due to heavy deposits of eumelanin.

Rump and Tail

The rump and uppertail coverts of the Gouldian Finch are blue, with the same combination of elements as the blue neck collar. The long tail feathers are black, the same as the flight feathers. The undertail coverts are an extension of the abdomen colour zone and are discussed in that section.

In effect, the blue of the neck collar, rump and tail coverts are all extensions of the back and wing plumage zone. They lack the presence of yellow lutein pigment and hence are blue instead of green.

Breast

The breast of the Gouldian Finch is a unique colour among birds, being a brilliant purple. Its method of production is quite different from similar colours in parrots because the Gouldian Finch is fortunate enough to have phaeomelanin present in its plumage. The breast feathers are structured just like the blue regions of plumage. The difference in colour is created because chestnut-red phaeomelanin replaces all the black eumelanin that is normally found in the medulla of blue feathers. The different melanin pigment alters the wavelength of light that is normally distorted by the feathers. The cloudy layer is still present and of equal importance, however the presence of phaeomelanin without eumelanin has great significance when it comes to the behaviour of different colour mutations. The breast region does not carry any carotenoid pigments, either yellow or red.

Belly

The belly region extends caudally into the undertail coverts. The main pigment present is yellow lutein which tends to fade and is less dense towards the tail of the bird. This region also carries small quantities of phaeomelanin, which is evident in Blue series birds. However there is no eumelanin present in this region.

Some specimens have a red line of canthaxanthin pigment adjoining the bottom of the purple breast area. This is known as the ***fusion bar*** and is viewed as desirable by many experienced breeders. Some of the earliest paintings of wild Gouldian Finches show the presence of a fusion bar.

Wild strain Black-headed Normal Gouldian Finch, insert showing a close-up of the fusion bar. The fusion bar was clearly indicated on most early paintings of wild Gouldian Finches. However, this feature has been generally lost from the domesticated bird.

MUTATIONS

HEAD COLOURS

There are two mutations that primarily change the colour of the head—the Black-headed and the Yellow-headed mutation. However only the Black-headed is a true head-colour mutation, whereas the Yellow-headed has a general action throughout the body. This is qualified by the fact that the Gouldian Finch has very little red pigment outside of the head region and therefore its action is not noticeable elsewhere.

Other colours are seen in the heads of Gouldian Finches, but they are the result of general-acting mutations and are often the combination of more than one mutation. It is therefore wrong to name these birds by a different head-colour name, as this creates the misconception that the change is brought about by a unique mutation and not merely as a feature of a mutation like the Blue or through various combinations.

Black-headed

Black-headed Normal Gouldian Finch cock (above) and hen (right).

The first mutation is a naturally occurring colour morph which actually outnumbers the true wildtype Red-headed Normal bird in wild populations. It only has one effect on the appearance of the bird—replacing the red colour of the head with black colouration.

The action of the gene is to alter the structure of the feathers of the head, removing their ability to carry carotenoid pigments. As a result the head region can no longer carry red canthaxanthin pigment and instead large quantities of black eumelanin are deposited in the altered feathers.

However the bird can still produce canthaxanthin pigment as evidenced by the red tip to the bill and the presence of red fusion bars in some specimens. It is a common mistake to think that this gene controls red pigment—a mistake unfortunately reinforced by a number of publications. The mistake was made because the wrong colour morph has been viewed as wildtype (see page 74 for further discussion).

The Black-headed mutation is sex-linked recessive. Because it prevents carotenoid pigment deposition in the head, it largely hides the presence of the Yellow-headed mutation in the bird. However, it is not epistatic towards Yellow-headed (ie it does not inactivate the gene) and this later gene is still able to function and alter the colour of the beak tip. This gene has no correlation to known mutations in other species of finches.

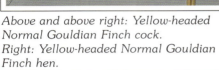

Above and above right: Yellow-headed Normal Gouldian Finch cock.
Right: Yellow-headed Normal Gouldian Finch hen.

Yellow-headed

The Yellow-headed mutation is also a naturally occurring colour morph of the Gouldian Finch. It also represents the most common mutation seen across all species of finches and is a direct correlation to the Yellow-billed Zebra Finch, the Yellow Star Finch, the Yellow Diamond Firetailed Finch, the Yellow Painted Firetail Finch, the Yellow Red-browed Finch and many other species of finches with a mutation that blocks production of red pigment in the bird.

Some debate occurs amongst breeders as to whether it should be called Yellow-headed or 'Orange-headed' and similar debate rages in other species like the Zebra Finch. Without heading into a debate about how these colours appear differently to different people, there is a simple reason why the region does not appear pure yellow despite the bird not being able to produce other carotenoid pigments. The reason is that melanin pigments are still present in the head region and these are creating the added 'orange' tone to the head.

These melanin pigments are visible in a Yellow-headed Blue series bird in the form of beige colouring in the head. The presence of these pigments can also be noted when certain melanin-altering mutations change the tone of the head from orange to a cleaner yellow colour in certain other combinations.

Yellow-headed Normal Gouldian Finch hen (left) and cock (right).

Above left and below: Black-headed Normal Gouldian Finch hen with yellow-tipped beak.

Above and left: Black-headed Normal Gouldian Finch cock with yellow-tipped beak.

Because the sole action of this mutation is to block production of red pigment at the yellow pigment stage, it is more appropriate to call this mutation Yellow-headed rather than 'Orange-headed'.

Like all 'yellow-billed' mutations, the Yellow-headed mutation is autosomal recessive. As mentioned previously, the Black-headed mutation largely blocks the visual appearance of the Yellow-headed mutation, but does not alter its action and the presence of the Yellow-headed gene can still be seen in the colour of the beak tip.

There has been recent work by Massa and Stradi (1999) and McGraw *et al* (2004) to investigate carotenoid pigments in passerines including Gouldian Finches. Massa and Stradi found that the Yellow-headed mutation carried both lutein (the base pigment in the diet) and 3'-dehydrolutein (a yellow metabolite produced via dehydrogenation) whereas Red-headed birds carry canthaxanthin (a 4-keto-carotenoid). Evidence indicates that the Yellow-headed locus codes for the ability to oxygenate the base carotenoids like lutein into the 4-keto-carotenoids (which are red) and when inactivated by the yellow-headed allele, only yellow metabolites can be produced. McGraw *et al* (2004) have demonstrated that this same process is present in other passerine species that normally produce red pigmentation but sometimes lose the ability through mutation, resulting in 'Yellowbill' colour morphs. This is extra confirmation that this colour morph in Gouldian Finches is a true Yellow-headed (Yellowbill) mutation rather than an 'Orange-headed' mutation.

BODY COLOUR

All other currently known colour mutations in Gouldian Finches act upon body colour and contrary to popular belief, actually act throughout the entire plumage. Currently there are no known pattern mutations in this species. Each of the body colour mutations acts upon a specific pigment in the plumage and performs this action anywhere the pigment is present. However, since the Gouldian Finch has different pigments in different plumage regions, many colour mutations appear to have action limited to one zone or another.

Blue

Left: Red-headed Blue Gouldian Finch cock.

Black-headed Blue Gouldian Finch cock (above) and hen (right).

The Blue mutation is common and distributed worldwide. It is variously also known as the 'Blue-backed' and the 'Blue-bodied' mutation, however it should more accurately be known merely as Blue. Like Blue mutations in parrots, it involves the loss of all yellow and related pigments throughout the entire plumage. The mode of inheritance is also the same—autosomal recessive.

Even though those pigments in Gouldian Finches are carotenoids and not the psittacofulvin pigments found in parrots, the action of the Blue mutation is basically the same. All yellows and reds are lost, thereby revealing any traces of melanin pigment that may have been hidden by those pigments. In its basic form (the Red-headed Blue), red pigment is removed from the head revealing phaeomelanin which gives the head a beige appearance. As a result, many breeders refer to these birds as 'Beige-headed' Blue, a misnomer which creates the possible misconception that some new 'Beige-headed' gene is in the make-up. Breeders should resist the desire to create new names for combinations and instead simply combine the names of the components.

The most obvious area of action for the Blue mutation is the back or body colour region. The gene prevents production of yellow pigments and when deleted from green plumage areas, a beautiful blue colour is produced. This mutation shows that the neck, rump and tail areas are confluent with the back and wings and the blue colouration is

Right: Juvenile Blue Gouldian Finch.
Below: A Yellow-headed Blue Gouldian Finch cannot be distinguished visually from a Red-headed Blue Gouldian Finch.
Below right: Red-headed Blue Gouldian Finch cock (left) and hen (right).

continuous without interruption through all of these zones. The Blue mutation also removes all yellow pigment from the belly region, once again revealing traces of phaeomelanin. However the purple of the breast is unaffected, confirming that carotenoids are not a significant component of the breast colour.

Blue is always a stunning mutation in any species of bird; however its value is greater than mere appearance as it helps reveal layers of melanin pigments not previously seen. And in combinations it adds to our understanding of the various melanin-altering mutations. When the Black-headed colour morph is added to the Blue there is no conflict. The Black-headed gene merely makes the head black, creating a stunning contrast with the rest of the bird.

Seagreen

Birds of this colour have appeared in various places around the world. In all instances it has proven difficult to establish. In theory, Seagreen should be both visually and genetically a Parblue. This means that it is a bird that has only lost a portion of the carotenoid pigment from the plumage, changing normal green colours to a blue-green (seagreen) colour. Genetically, the mutation should also be autosomal recessive and would be a Partial Blue gene, belonging to the same locus—in essence a partially effective 'blue' gene.

Red-headed Seagreen Gouldian Finch cock.

All this means is that when a Seagreen is mated to a Blue, the expected outcome should be part way in colour between the two mutations and not a Normal Green double split for the two mutations.

Right and far right: Black-headed Seagreen Gouldian Finch hen.

However, there is a colour morph in parrotfinches (the Seagreen Red-headed Parrotfinch) which is sex-linked recessive and clearly a completely different type of gene. Because of its inheritance, the parrotfinch mutation is not a true Seagreen mutation, despite being visually what we would expect of a true Seagreen. There is also a third possibility for the Seagreen Gouldian Finch. It may be an acquired colour, as there are some reports of the birds moulting into normal green plumage over time. Until the Seagreen Gouldian Finch is established and its genetic inheritance proven, it is impossible to guess exactly what the colour really is.

Visually, Seagreen shows typical Parblue features, with carotenoid pigments partially reduced in all areas. As mentioned already, the green back colour of the Normal bird becomes blue-green. However, there are changes in the belly colour, which becomes a lighter, creamier yellow. The head colour is also reduced in the Red-headed and Yellow-headed forms.

Sex-linked Pastel (Yellow-backed)

This mutation is common and available worldwide. It is also associated with more poor naming choices than any other mutation that I am aware of in aviculture. Some of this is possibly brought about by its unique status in aviculture, being the only sex-linked co-dominant mutation currently established. Therefore no equivalent mutation exists in other finch or parrot species with

Above and right: Red-headed DF Pastel Green Gouldian Finch cock.

Red-headed SF Pastel Green Gouldian Finch cock.

Left: Red-headed DF Pastel Green Gouldian Finch cock.
Below: Red-headed SF Pastel Green Gouldian Finch hen.

which to set a naming precedent. However most of the naming mess stems from the practice of giving every different gene combination a different name.

To begin with, the mutation has been given a different name in virtually every different country in which it is found. It is variously known as 'Yellow-backed', 'Yellow', European 'Dilute' and Pastel. In many instances it is given different names for single and double factor versions (eg Green Pastel and Yellow Pastel in Europe) with the hen being named differently again. These are changed yet again when other mutations like Blue and White-breasted are added to the mix, introducing names like 'Silver' and 'Yellow-bodied'.

For breeders to have any chance of understanding what kind of mutation they have, a single consistent name needs to be chosen for the mutation and it needs to be applied consistently no matter what the circumstances are.

Black-headed DF Pastel Green Gouldian Finch cock.

Red-headed SF Pastel Green (left) and Black-headed SF Pastel Green Gouldian Finch hens.

Black-headed SF Pastel Green Gouldian Finch cock.

1. Black-headed SF Pastel Green Gouldian Finch hen.
2. Black-headed SF Pastel Green Gouldian Finch hen.
3. Yellow-headed SF Pastel Green Gouldian Finch hen.
4. Yellow-headed DF Pastel Green Gouldian Finch cock.
5. A Pastel Gouldian Finch chick just fledged has a definite yellow tone to its colour.
6. Yellow-headed SF Pastel Green Gouldian Finch cock.
7. Yellow-headed SF Pastel Green Gouldian Finch cock (left) showing reduced black bib and pencil lines compared to a Yellow-headed Normal Gouldian Finch cock.
8. Black-headed DF Pastel Green Gouldian Finch cock.

1 & 4. Red-headed SF Pastel Blue Gouldian Finch cock.
2 & 3. Red-headed DF Pastel Blue Gouldian Finch cock.

At this point in time, Pastel is possibly the best choice as it is already in common use in Europe as well as being used for a sex-linked diluting gene in canaries and Java Sparrows, albeit one that works via a different genetic process. Alternatively, 'Yellow-backed' would be a satisfactory name if breeders could accept using it in combinations like Double Factor Yellow-backed Blue for a silvery white-coloured bird. The terms 'Yellow' and 'Dilute' should not be used for this mutation (in any combination) to try and reduce the breeder confusion that currently exists with this bird and the Australian Yellow and Dilute-backed Gouldian Finch mutations. Particularly in Europe and the USA, many breeders do not realise that these two unique Gouldian Finch mutations even exist in Australia, because their names are so commonly misused for the Sex-linked Pastel mutation.

While looking for comparatives in other species of finches one mutation warrants discussion—the Florida Fancy Zebra Finch. This mutation is also co-dominant, although

Left and above: Red-headed SF Pastel Blue Gouldian Finch hen.

Black-headed SF Pastel Blue Gouldian Finch cock.

Black-headed SF Pastel Blue Gouldian Finch hen.

Black-headed DF Pastel Blue Gouldian Finch cock.

autosomal instead of sex-linked. Yet the other similarities between the two mutations are very evident. In the double factor forms, both mutations remove virtually all eumelanin, but have no action on phaeomelanin. And in single factor form a phenotype is produced that is roughly halfway between the normal and the double-factored bird. Unfortunately the Zebra Finch mutation does not offer any naming options, yet the similar action of the two mutations is worth noting and comparing.

The sex-linked Pastel mutation acts upon only one pigment in the plumage of the Gouldian Finch. It almost completely blocks the production of eumelanin. Being co-dominant, the single factor cock has one wildtype gene to increase the amount of pigment produced. Double-factored cocks show the full expression of the mutation which is almost total suppression of eumelanin. Because the hen only has one X chromosome and a Y chromosome, she only comes in one colour morph. This is similar to the double-factored cock as, like him, she does not carry a wildtype gene to increase the pigment production.

Eumelanin is most prominent in the head and body colour regions of the bird. In the wildtype Red-headed Gouldian Finch, the areas of the plumage affected are the bib, pencil line, neck, back, wing and tail colours. Black markings like the bib, pencil lines, flight and tail feathers are greatly reduced in colour to a light grey in single factor cocks and lose virtually all pigment (but not quite white) in the double factor cock. Green and blue areas of plumage are equally affected, being lightened in colour in two steps towards yellow and white, but not attaining a clean colour due to the presence of phaeomelanin in all areas.

As the breast colour is produced by phaeomelanin, this mutation has no effect in this area. Similarly it does not alter belly colour which is yellow carotenoid combined with small amounts of phaeomelanin.

The Black-headed Pastel combination results in the head colour changing to eumelanin, which is then acted upon by the Pastel gene. This results in a medium grey head colour in single factor cocks and an almost white head colour in hens and double factor cocks. The rest of the plumage is the same as for a Red-headed Pastel.

When combined with the Blue mutation, the colour should be referred to as Single Factor or Double Factor Pastel Blue, rather than using different terms for the different combinations of genes. It has been common for breeders to only refer to the single factor form as Pastel Blue and to call the double factor form by the term 'Silver'. While I can understand why there is a desire to call the later birds 'Silver', this name should be reserved for the future when a Grey Factor appears and will turn this combination into a true silver colour.

Dilute-backed

Red-headed Dilute-backed Gouldian Finch cock.

Above and right: Red-headed Dilute-backed Gouldian Finch hen.

Outside of Australia, this mutation is unknown. It is also commonly misunderstood and generally considered by non-Australian breeders to be synonymous with the Sex-linked Pastel (Yellow-backed) mutation. Visually it is similar to but a bit lighter than the Single Factor Pastel cock. However beyond this superficial similarity in appearance, we find that the genetics and behaviour of this mutation are completely different.

The similar appearance is due to both mutations acting solely upon eumelanin pigment. However, while the Pastel is sex-linked co-dominant, the Dilute-backed is autosomal recessive. This means that there is only one phenotype for the Dilute-backed compared to multiple phenotypes for the Pastel. And if we compare the full expression of the two different mutations, the Double Factor Pastel and the Dilute-backed, we find quite different degrees of expression. The Dilute-backed only ever reduces eumelanin to approximately 50% of normal.

This results in diluted colours for markings and body colour, with no effect on breast or belly colour and no effect on carotenoids in the head colour. Pencil lines, flight and tail feathers become medium grey and the green back colour is reduced significantly.

Technically, this mutation is not a true Dilute for two reasons. It begins life with a reddish eye colour that darkens quickly as the chick grows. This is a feature of albinism, not dilution.

Red-headed Dilute-backed Gouldian Finch cocks.

Page 89

1 & 2. Black-headed Dilute-backed Gouldian Finch hen.
3. Juvenile Dilute-backed Gouldian Finches are a light creamy colour.
4. Black-headed Dilute-backed Green Gouldian Finch cock.
5. Nest of Dilute-backed chicks showing lighter pigmentation including eye colour.
6. Yellow-headed Dilute-backed Gouldian Finch cock.
7. Yellow-headed Dilute-backed Gouldian Finch cock.
8. Yellow-headed Dilute-backed Gouldian Finch hen.

Secondly, true Dilutes alter both melanin types, whereas this mutation only alters eumelanin production. However, it is not easy to place this mutation in an existing mutation category due to a lack of examples in other finch species.

Some European breeders have suggested that it might be an Isabel mutation, however the degree of eumelanin reduction is insufficient for Isabel and the eyes darken too quickly in the chick. Isabel mutations have reddish eyes even as adults and also virtually eliminate all eumelanin, leaving only faint brown tones instead of the natural black-grey tone of eumelanin.

There is only one mutation that I know of in another species that appears to correlate with the Dilute-backed Gouldian Finch—the Australian mutation of the Zebra Finch known as Slate. In Zebra Finches, this mutation has also been known as 'Recessive Dilute', which ties in with the name used in Gouldian Finches. Like the Dilute-backed Gouldian Finch, the Slate Zebra Finch is a dark albinistic mutation, reducing black areas of plumage to a medium grey colour.

The Dilute-backed Gouldian Finch mutation produces some interesting combinations with other mutations, the results differing significantly from similar combinations involving the sex-linked Pastel mutation. The reason is that different mutations work at different points in the process of pigment production and therefore interact with each other in slightly different ways.

Yellow (Australian Yellow)

This mutation also has a degree of confusion associated with it, particularly outside of its country of origin. In fact it is still unknown outside of Australia, although reports from the USA indicate that a 'Recessive Yellow' is under development there. The Australian Yellow is an autosomal recessive mutation that blocks both eumelanin and phaeomelanin. The resultant phenotype is similar to the White-breasted Pastel combination, leading many overseas breeders to think that the Yellow has something to do with the White-breasted mutation, which it does not. It is natural for differing melanin-altering mutations to appear similar, yet each has peculiarities associated with how their genes function.

The Australian Yellow mutation is the true Black-eyed Yellow mutation in the Gouldian Finch. It is directly equivalent to the White Zebra Finch and even shares the common feature of having a 'dirty' mantle area in chicks and young birds.

Yellow-headed Australian Yellow Gouldian Finch cock.

Black-eyed Clear mutations act upon the melanocytes themselves, possibly interfering with melanoblast migration

Nest of Australian Yellow (far left and right) and Normal Gouldian Finch chicks showing black eyes from hatch.

Australian White (left) and Normal Gouldian Finch nestlings. The Australian White shows blue 'foul' feathering on the back.

Page 91

Some breeders are now increasing the 'foul feathering' and producing birds like these three examples.

Above: Black-headed Australian Yellow hen with heavily marked mantle.
Left: Red-headed Australian Yellow cock with heavily marked mantle.
Far left: 'Foul feathers' are commonly seen in Australian Yellow Gouldian Finches like this Red-headed cock.

throughout the skin in the embryo. If the skin lacks melanocytes, there are no cells to produce melanin of either type. However, wherever the cells reach there is fully functional melanin production. Hence the eyes of this mutation remain black and do not change to red, ruby or plum.

Australian breeders have traditionally referred to this mutation as 'Australian White-breasted Yellow' which no doubt added to the confusion with other mutations. To avoid this problem, it is important that the name be shortened to its simplest accurate identification. Yellow is appropriate because this is the expected phenotype for the Black-eyed Clear and other mutations will only imitate it through combinations.

European breeders may prefer to call this mutation a 'Recessive Pied' because so many of the young retain areas of melanin pigmentation. However, I resist this idea for a number of reasons. Firstly, we can expect that one of the many typical Pied mutations will occur in Gouldian Finches and be established at some time in the future. And as we see in the Zebra Finch, there are significant differences in appearance between a White (the Clear mutation) and a Pied. Secondly, I doubt that any Black-eyed Clear mutation (as distinct from combination colours) can produce absolute leucism in 100% of individuals—or at least it is extremely rare. Thirdly, breeders of this mutation naturally strive towards a Clear phenotype, rather than a Pied phenotype. Hence the reason why most Australian breeders instinctively called this colour 'Yellow'. We are unlikely to see another primary mutation produce a cleaner Black-eyed Yellow phenotype than this mutation.

Red-headed Australian Yellow hen.

As mentioned previously, the action of the mutation is to block all melanin production throughout the plumage, leaving only the red and yellow carotenoid pigments. This results in green regions like the back and the wings becoming yellow.

Australian White Gouldian Finch—a true Black-eyed White.

The melanin retention in this bird is so great that it retains much of its purple chest colour.

Red-headed Australian Yellow cock with clear yellow back.

Black markings like the pencil lines, the bib and the tail become white. The yellow of the belly and the red of the head are unaffected, although the colours may appear cleaner as the phaeomelanin pigment is removed. The chest becomes white because phaeomelanin is lost, leaving no pigment for the structural colour to work against. It is most important to stress that the white breast colour is an action of this mutation alone and not as a result of a second mutation (the White-breasted) being combined with it.

Following the conventions used for Canary and Zebra Finch exhibitions, the areas of melanin retention seen in many birds should be referred to as 'foul markings' or 'foul feathers'.

This mutation should only be combined with Black-headed, Yellow-headed and Blue colour mutations. In the Black-headed Yellow combination, the Yellow mutation removes all pigment from the head, resulting in a 'white-headed' yellow colour. The action of the Yellow-headed gene is unaffected by the Yellow mutation, being mutually exclusive in action, therefore the combination produces a straightforward Yellow-headed Yellow. Combining the Blue mutation with the Yellow mutation results in a Black-eyed White Gouldian Finch because, between them, the two genes block all pigments produced by the bird, except for a few foul feathers left by the Yellow mutation. Combination with any of the melanin-altering mutations is pointless and merely results in confusion about future breeding results.

White-breasted

The White-breasted mutation would be the most common colour morph worldwide, after the two wild colour morphs and has been readily combined with many other mutations. Its inheritance is autosomal recessive.

Despite being named because of its white breast (the most obvious feature of its appearance), the action of this mutation occurs throughout the entire plumage. For evidence of this, we only need consider how other areas of plumage change when it is combined with mutations like the sex-linked Pastel and the recessive Dilute-backed. To understand why, we need to consider exactly what the action of this gene is.

Red-headed White-breasted Green Gouldian Finch cock.

1. Yellow-headed White-breasted Green Gouldian Finch hen.
2. Juvenile White-breasted Normal Gouldian Finch hen.
3. Red-headed White-breasted Green Gouldian Finch cock.
4. Red-headed White-breasted Green Gouldian Finch hen.
5. Black-headed White-breasted Green Gouldian Finch hen.
6. Black-headed White-breasted Green Gouldian Finch cock.
7. Yellow-headed White-breasted Green Gouldian Finch cock.

Some authors have theorised that the feather structure of the breast feathers was somehow altered, but this would not change the breast to white. Instead we would see a reddish brown colour—the appearance of phaeomelanin. The true action of the White-breasted gene is to block phaeomelanin production throughout the plumage, or more specifically to 'redirect the phaeomelanin into eumelanin'.

Red-headed White-breasted Blue Gouldian Finch hen (left) and cock (below).

This last comment will confuse many people, because surely that action would change the breast to blue or perhaps black or grey. However that does not happen because the Gouldian Finch has other genes that independently restrict eumelanin from the breast and belly regions, which is why it does not naturally have any eumelanin in this region to begin with. It therefore does not matter that the White-breasted gene is producing eumelanin, because that pigment is blocked and the result is a white breast region devoid of all melanin.

Why is this distinction important? Because when the White-breasted gene is combined with other melanin-altering mutations, unexpected results can occur. For instance, when combined with the sex-linked Pastel gene, it complements the Pastel mutation's blockage of eumelanin, resulting in a phenotype that has greater reduction of both melanin types. In simpler words, the plumage becomes closer to yellow.

Yet when combined with the Dilute-backed mutation we see a completely different outcome, an increase in eumelanin pigments in the combination bird compared with the base Dilute-backed phenotype. Perhaps the White-breasted gene redirects the melanin pathway 'around' the Dilute-backed gene, or alternatively it may inhibit the second gene in some way.

While the exact action of this gene can only be speculated upon at this time, what is certain is that it is the direct equivalent of a number of mutations known in other finch species including Grey Bengalese Finches, Grey Long-tailed Grassfinches and Black-cheeked Zebra Finches. Each of these other mutations also redirects phaeomelanin pathways back into the eumelanin pathway, therefore removing all phaeomelanin from the plumage.

Black-headed White-breasted Blue Gouldian Finch hen (above) and cock (right).

Examples of Lilac-breasted Gouldian Finch mutations.

1. Red-headed Lilac-breasted Green Gouldian Finch cock.
2. Black-headed Lilac-breasted Green Gouldian Finch cock.
3. & 4. Black-headed Lilac-breasted Green Gouldian Finch hen.
5. Yellow-headed Lilac-breasted Green Gouldian Finch cock.
6. Red-headed Lilac-breasted Green Gouldian Finch hen.
7. Yellow-headed Lilac-breasted Green Gouldian Finch cock.

Lilac-breasted

Lilac-breasted Gouldian Finches are commonly bred worldwide, although not well established everywhere. The mutation is autosomal recessive and is believed to form a multiple allelic series with the White-breasted mutation. In effect it is a 'partially acting White-breasted' gene, producing a reduced quantity of phaeomelanin compared to Normal but not blocking it completely like the White-breasted mutation.

With its apparent action, it would be logical that it were a multiple allele with the White-breasted mutation and indeed most breeding results suggest that this is the case, although doubts still exist for some breeders. Because of the allelic series, the mutation will behave as though dominant to White-breasted, while being recessive to Normal.

Above: Black-headed Lilac-breasted Blue Gouldian Finch cock.
Above right: Red-headed Lilac-breasted Blue Gouldian Finch cock.

Its action allows it to combine effectively with virtually all mutations in Gouldian Finches except the Australian Yellow and of course it cannot be combined with the White-breasted allele.

RARE MUTATIONS

The following mutations and colours are only held in small numbers in one region of the world. They are either new, proving difficult to establish or have uncertain inheritance patterns.

Blue-breasted

Blue-breasted Gouldian Finches are well reported, but are yet to be established as a true breeding mutation. To create a blue breast colour on a Gouldian Finch, you need to convert the phaeomelanin deep in the chest region into eumelanin. This is achieved with the White-breasted mutation; however other genes still block production of the eumelanin. In certain strains of White-breasted, this suppression of eumelanin fails and blue patches of colour begin to appear.

Therefore to produce blue chest colour, we need a minimum of two mutations—one gene to convert into eumelanin and one gene to prevent it being suppressed. Therefore it is not surprising that it is a difficult colour to establish. I would recommend anyone trying to reproduce this colour, to try using White-breasted birds to help establish the mutation.

Red-headed White-breasted Green cock showing a blue band along the bottom of the breast area. The blue colour confirms that phaeomelanin is converted to eumelanin in the White-breasted mutation. Birds like this may lead to a Blue-breasted mutation.

Cinnamon

The Cinnamon mutation has been bred regularly in Europe over the past decade but is yet to be firmly established. The name 'Cinnamon' has sometimes been used incorrectly in Australia for other colours, which is unfortunate because the true Cinnamon gene is one of the most common mutations across all species of birds and deserves to be accurately identified. Photographs of the European Cinnamon Gouldian Finch indicate that it has been correctly identified and its typical sex-linked recessive inheritance confirms this.

The action of the Cinnamon gene is quite simple. It prevents final conversion of brown eumelanin into black eumelanin. This results in all black areas of the plumage appearing as a shade of brown. Because the eumelanin throughout the plumage is altered, green and blue colours are also affected but there is only a slight reduction in their tone. The brown markings are most evident in the Black-headed Cinnamon combination, but are also evident in the pencil lines and the flight and tail feathers of Red-headed Cinnamon Gouldian Finches.

The Cinnamon gene has no effect on phaeomelanin production; therefore the breast colour is unchanged. In combination with other mutations it acts independently, however gene interactions may be expected with the sex-linked Lutino and perhaps other albinistic mutations.

Above: Black-headed Normal (left) and Black-headed Cinnamon Gouldian Finch hens. This photograph highlights the dark brown head of the Cinnamon bird. Left: Black-headed Cinnamon Gouldian Finch hen.

Cinnamon mutations would combine best with the head-colour mutations and the Blue mutation as well as the darker melanin-reducing mutations such as the Dilute-backed and the Single Factor Pastel.

Japanese 'Red-eye Factor' (Fallow)

Communications with Japanese breeders indicate the presence in that country of a 'Red-eyed' Normal mutation for a number of decades. However it has only ever existed in small numbers and has a reputation for lacking vigour. Photographs posted on a number of Japanese web sites confirm the existence of this mutation. The most obvious colour change is in the eye colour which is often described by breeders as being 'wine-coloured'. There is also an overall reduction in melanin, resulting in a

Japanese-bred 'Albino' and 'Lutino' chicks.

A Japanese 'Albino' Gouldian Finch created by combining Blue with their 'Lutino' lookalike.

Three Japanese 'Albino' Gouldian Finches.

slightly lighter plumage colouration than Normal. These features, in conjunction with an autosomal recessive mode of inheritance, point to this being a Fallow mutation.

Perhaps unfortunately for this mutation, it has mostly been combined with other mutations, the aim being to produce a 'Lutino'-coloured bird. I say 'unfortunately' because it deserves recognition in its own right as a unique mutation that requires a concerted effort to establish in its pure form. And this problem has been compounded by the establishment of true Lutino mutations in both Europe and the USA. If the Lutino is imported into Japan and bred through the 'Red-eyed' birds, then it would be easy for the Fallow mutation to be lost for ever. There are reports that some 'Red-eyed' birds have been imported into the USA from Japan and it is hoped that breeders there will recognise it as a unique mutation worthy of breeding in its own right.

Japanese breeders have produced a 'Lutino' Gouldian Finch by combining three or more mutations, but the Fallow ('Red-eye Factor') remains rare in its pure form.

As mentioned above, Japanese breeders have used the Fallow gene to create the first 'Lutino' and 'Albino' Gouldian Finches in the world, although the birds produced are only mimics of the true 'single gene' Lutino that is now established elsewhere. They did this by combining the Fallow, sex-linked Pastel and White-breasted mutations to produce a bird indistinguishable from Lutino. They then added the Blue mutation to produce a bird identical to Albino in colour.

Lutino

The true sex-linked Lutino mutation has now been established independently in both Belgium and the USA. The European strain shows very slight retention of eumelanin primarily in the head region of Black-headed birds, while the USA strain shows slight retention of phaeomelanin primarily in the breast region of the plumage. In each instance it is not unexpected as no Lutino mutation is absolute in its loss of melanin. The body simply cannot function without at least a trace of melanin production. What is interesting is that these two mutations are almost certainly alleles, but represent two separate

1. Close-up of head of a Yellowtip Bill Black-headed Lutino Gouldian Finch hen.
2. Two nestling USA Lutino Gouldian Finch chicks.
3. Hatchling USA Lutino Gouldian Finch chicks.
4 & 5. European Black-headed Lutino hen.
6. European Yellow-headed Lutino hen.
7. European Albino Gouldian Finch hen.
8. Yellowtip Bill Black-headed Lutino Gouldian Finch hen of the USA strain.

mutations of the same gene locus. Care will be needed in the future to ensure the independent survival of the two mutations.

Temptation may also exist to produce a 'better' Lutino through combination with other mutations such as the White-breasted for the USA strain and the Pastel for the Belgian strain. While there is no harm in this experimentation, it is important that the original mutations are not lost in their true identity and any combinations produced correctly identified as combinations.

Redtip Bill Black-headed Lutino (left and centre) and Yellowtip Bill Black-headed Lutino Gouldian Finches. The USA strain shows slight retention of phaeomelanin in the breast region, which varies in appearance depending on photographic conditions.

Dark Factor

Perhaps the most exciting mutation of recent years has been the establishment of the Dark Factor mutation by breeders in the UK. This mutation is co-dominant and is directly comparable with the Dark Factor mutation in parrots, producing Dark Green and Olive colours. When combined with the Blue mutation, it produces Cobalt and Mauve colours.

This mutation works by altering the feather structure, changing the frequency of light distortion produced through constructive interference. It does not add pigment as commonly thought. In altering the feather structure, we know from parrots that often the feather quality suffers to some degree as well. It is important therefore to select for good feather quality with this mutation.

I call this mutation exciting because scientists have shown that the mechanism of light distortion in Gouldian Finches is the same as in parrots.

Above: Red-headed Dark Green (left) and Yellow-headed Green cocks illustrating the effect of the Dark Factor on the Gouldian Finch. Right: Red-headed Dark Green Gouldian Finch cock.

Now with the appearance of this mutation we have evidence that they also share similar genetic control of feather structure. One day in the near future when we can DNA sequence these genes, it will be interesting to find out if these two disparate families of birds share common genes, perhaps indicating a common ancestor in past millennia. The other exciting thing about this mutation is its potential for combination with other mutations to produce a whole new range of colours. Only combinations with Lutino and Australian Yellow would be pointless as these mutations do not leave sufficient melanin for the production of structural colouration.

'Lime'

From left to right: Redtip Bill Black-headed 'Lime' hen, Yellowtip Bill Black-headed 'Lime' hen and Black-headed Normal cock Gouldian Finches. The contrast in black colouration is quite noticeable in this photograph.

I have recently been privileged to see a new Australian mutation under development in Gouldian Finches. At first glance the casual observer may not notice this new colour in a mixed aviary, but once the telltale features are realised it is quite an attractive colour and well deserves to be established and propagated. And then there is also the potential for new knowledge to be gained through its combination with other mutations, in particular the White-breasted.

This mutation is probably inherited as a sex-linked recessive gene, although the sex linkage has not been confirmed beyond doubt at this stage. Consideration of the inheritance and the phenotypic appearance of this bird may lead breeders to confuse it with the Cinnamon mutation. Indeed the body colour of the two mutations is quite similar and because neither has any effect on phaeomelanin, the breast colour is normal in both. However, close observation of the head colour shows it to be dull sooty black in the 'Lime' bird whereas the Cinnamon bird has a dark chocolate-brown head in Black-headed specimens (assess the pencil lines and the bib in Red-headed and Yellow-headed birds). The tail and flight feathers also show a difference, the 'Lime' having

Above: Normal (left) and 'Lime' chicks at pin-feather stage. The 'Lime' chick clearly shows reduced melanin in the bill, skin and pin-stage flight feathers. Right: Yellowtip Bill Black-headed 'Lime' Gouldian Finch hen. The head is a dull sooty black colour.

Yellowtip Bill Black-headed 'Lime' hen. Note the grey tones of the tail feathers and the slightly reduced back colour.

lighter grey tone feathers compared to Normal and the Cinnamon having clear brown colours in these areas.

Considering the genetic identity of this new mutation, if it does prove to be sex-linked, there is only one locus it could belong to—the ino locus. If this proves correct, it would be a Parino mutation, the genetic equivalent to Pallid or Lime in parrots and equivalent to Agate in canaries, although perhaps with slightly greater levels of melanin retention. Test mating this mutation with the sex-linked Lutino gene may prove this theory. However, as the two mutations currently only exist on different continents, this will not happen any time soon. In the meantime we can only speculate upon the true identity of this new colour and wait to see what happens as breeders establish it in aviculture and eventually combine it into new colours.

Turquoise ('Australian Blue')

There is a strain of 'Blue' Gouldian Finches which began in Western Australia around the same time as the Blue mutation originating from Europe began to appear in Australia. As a result, few breeders paid much attention to the birds from Western Australia, considering them to be the same as other Blue Gouldians Finches available at the time. However, the visual difference in these birds has recently been drawn to my attention. In the Red-headed specimens photographed, the ventral area of the bird appears to have 100% carotenoid reduction. It has lost the red tip to the bill, the red from the head and all yellow lutein has been lost from the belly. Yet when you consider the back colour, it is not the same shade of blue that we find in the true Blue mutation. It has more of a greenish blue tone.

I believe that this strain of 'Blue' Gouldian might prove to be a Turquoise mutation. Turquoise is used to describe Parblue mutations which are close to true Blue in colour, but which still retain small amounts of yellow pigment. Another feature of Turquoise mutations is that they have an uneven reduction of yellow pigments. Comparing this to the Seagreen mutation which retains some lutein evenly throughout the plumage, this

A possible Turquoise mutation in the Red-headed Gouldian Finch that has been referred to as 'Australian Blue' in the past.

The possible Turquoise mutation in the Gouldian Finch has a more greenish blue tone to its back colour, in contrast to the Blue mutation of European origin.

Turquoise mutation completely reduces lutein (and canthaxanthin) in the head, breast and belly regions while there appears to be significant retention of lutein in the back.

To confirm or refute this proposal, these birds must first be established as a breeding strain free from the established Blue mutation. Next, combination with melanin-reducing mutations can be used to visualise whether any lutein remains in the plumage.

A combination of White-breasted DF Pastel Turquoise should produce a bird with a light yellow back and a white breast and belly. Alternatively, feathers from the mutation would need to be investigated microscopically to determine which pigments were still present.

I would expect a Turquoise mutation to be inherited as autosomal recessive and form a multiple allelic series with Seagreen and Blue. As the likelihood of confusion is great if any of these three genes are combined, it would be desirable to keep them are pure breeding strains separate from each other, until controlled scientific studies can be undertaken.

Above: A possible new 'Dilute' mutation.

'Dilute'

A new mutation has been bred in Australia that for now is referred to as 'Dilute'. Its exact identity will not be certain until it is fully established. It appears to be autosomal recessive in inheritance.

'Grey Factor'

I have received reports and seen occasional photographs of birds that may be Greygreen, representing the development of a Grey Factor mutation. At this time I cannot be certain as the photographs left some doubts and I have not seen the birds first-hand. If it is indeed a Grey Factor, it will allow the production of Grey Gouldian Finches, as well as combining with other mutations like Cinnamon to eventually produce fawn colours. I would expect a Grey Factor to be dominant in inheritance, although a few examples of recessive Greygreen are known in parrot species.

'White-wing'

In the USA, breeders have produced a number of birds with 'white' or pale wing colours. Some birds of this strain also show 'pied' areas on the back of the head, but without the pale wing colour. It is not currently known whether there is a direct link between these features, nor is it certain if these birds represent a new mutation or simply a colour variation.

A Red-headed SF Pastel Blue Gouldian Finch cock showing the 'White-wing' variation being bred by breeders in the USA.

COLOUR COMBINATIONS

It is popular for breeders to refer to combination colours as 'secondary mutations' even though this is incorrect and misleading. The word 'mutation' refers directly to the genetic change that has happened within a bird. Therefore a 'secondary mutation' is a mutant gene that has mutated for a second time, which is a rare event. That is quite different from a bird carrying two different mutant genes that have been combined through selective breeding. The former is a random event we cannot control, the latter is an engineered event brought about by humans.

Unfortunately, most modern avicultural writers use the word 'mutation' incorrectly as a synonym for 'colour' or 'phenotype'. So this has led easily into the inaccurate terminology of 'secondary mutations'.

The production of colour combinations is an important process because it opens up the range of colours, increasing the numbers of colours exponentially as each new mutation appears. Yet, while every new gene could be combined with each older pre-existing mutation, not every combination is attractive nor wise.

When considering if two mutations might produce a distinctive combination, it is best

Below left: Yellow-headed White-breasted SF Pastel Green Gouldian Finch cock.
Below centre: Red-headed White-breasted SF Pastel Green Gouldian Finch cock
Below right: Yellow-headed White-breasted SF Pastel Green Gouldian Finch cock.

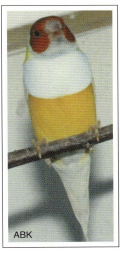

Above: Yellow-headed White-breasted SF Pastel Green Gouldian Finch cock.
Left: Red-headed White-breasted SF Pastel Green Gouldian Finch hen.

to consider which elements of pigmentation are altered by the mutation. The best combinations are of mutations that act upon different pigments within the plumage. For instance, those that alter carotenoid pigments like the Blue and Seagreen mutations combine well with any melanin-altering mutation such as Pastel or Dilute-backed.

If differing components are affected, then a new colour will be produced but if the same element is changed, then one mutation may mask the other. For instance, the Blue mutation eliminates production of carotenoids and therefore leaves no pigment for the Yellow-headed gene to act upon. As a result, Red-headed Blue and Yellow-headed Blue are visually indistinguishable. We say that the Blue gene masks the presence of the Yellow-headed gene.

Similarly, strong melanin-reducing mutations like Lutino or Australian Yellow do not leave significant melanin in the plumage for other melanin-altering mutations to act upon and combinations of these colours with mutations like Pastel, White-breasted or Dilute-backed have little real value, the exception being for limited scientific investigation.

1 & 3. Red-headed White-breasted SF Pastel Blue Gouldian Finch cock.
2. Red-headed White-breasted DF Pastel Blue Gouldian Finch cock.
4. Black-headed White-breasted SF Pastel Blue Gouldian Finch hen.
5. Black-headed White-breasted DF Pastel Blue Gouldian Finch cock.
6. Black-headed White-breasted SF Pastel Blue Gouldian Finch cock.

Presently, Gouldian breeders are lucky because most of the available mutations can be combined effectively to create new colours. And there is the added dimension brought about by melanin-altering mutations being divisible into eumelanin-altering, phaeomelanin-altering and dual melanin-altering mutations. Many intriguing outcomes are produced by combining the phaeomelanin-altering White-breasted mutation with eumelanin-altering mutations like Pastel and Dilute-backed.

Yet the most exciting combinations are still to come, once new mutations like Dark Factor become readily available. This mutation alters structure and combines well with any mutation

1 & 2. Red-headed Dilute-backed Blue Gouldian Finch cocks.
3. Black-headed Lilac-breasted SF Pastel Green Gouldian Finch cock.
4. Red-headed Lilac-breasted SF Pastel Blue Gouldian Finch cock. Lilac-breasted interacts with Pastel in a similar but lesser way than White-breasted does.
5. Yellow-headed Lilac-breasted SF Pastel Green Gouldian Finch cock.
6. Red-headed Lilac-breasted DF Pastel Green Gouldian Finch cock.
7. Black-headed Lilac-breasted DF Pastel Green Gouldian Finch cock.

that retains sufficient melanin for it to work with, thereby adding many new shades of greens and blues to the range we now have.

Who knows, if we are lucky, one day perhaps even a Violet Factor may appear.

1. Black-headed White-breasted Seagreen Gouldian Finch cock (left) and Black-headed White-breasted Blue Gouldian Finch cock (right)—highlighting that Seagreen is a Parblue-type mutation.
2. Red-headed White-breasted Seagreen Gouldian Finch cock.
3. Black-headed White-breasted Blue Gouldian Finch cock (left) and Black-headed White-breasted Seagreen Gouldian Finch cock (right)—further highlighting the Parblue features of the Seagreen.
4. Black-headed Blue Gouldian Finch hen (left) and Black-headed Dark Blue (Cobalt) Gouldian Finch hen (right). The Dark Factor opens up many new possibilities in Gouldian Finch mutations.
5. Black-headed White-breasted Seagreen hen.

White-breasted Combinations

The White-breasted mutation deserves a special chapter of its own on its combinations with other mutations. This is because the White-breasted gene acts upon phaeomelanin, converting it into eumelanin. While this will be merely masked by the few genes that totally block both melanin types, such as the Australian Yellow and Lutino mutations, it produces intriguing results when combined with mutations that only alter eumelanin. ('Masking' is the process whereby one mutation completely hides the presence of another mutation.)

To understand the results produced, you need to first understand the basic process of melanin production. Roughly speaking, melanin pigmentation can be divided into three basic components that correlate to the main categories of melanin-altering mutations. Firstly, cells are required to produce the pigment. These are called melanocytes and their behaviour and cellular functions, including migration in the embryo, are controlled by a number of genes. Mutation of one of these genes will produce leucistic mutations, which include the Australian Yellow and a number of Pied mutations. Secondly, the two different melanin pigments must be produced through metabolic pathways within the **melanocyte**, controlled by a number of genes. Mutations of these metabolic genes produce albinistic mutations, which are the largest group of mutations in Gouldian Finches and other avicultural species as well. Finally the pigment must be transferred from the melanocyte into the growing feather and this is controlled by a couple of genes alone. Mutations of one of these genes produce the true Dilutes which are rare and currently do not exist in Gouldian Finches.

The White-breasted gene acts upon the phaeomelanin pathway so we need to know more about the metabolism of both melanin types. Melanin production begins with an amino acid called tyrosine and an enzyme called tyrosinase. After a few metabolic steps eumelanin and phaeomelanin pathways diverge until the final products are produced. As a result, mutations of the genes that control early steps in the process will alter both pigment types; however mutations of later steps only act upon one of the two parallel pathways. Pastel, Dilute-backed and Cinnamon mutations act

1. Black-headed White-breasted Dilute-backed Green Gouldian Finch cock.
2. Red-headed White-breasted Dilute-backed Green Gouldian Finch cock.
3. Red-headed White-breasted Dilute-backed Green Gouldian Finch hen.

Red-headed White-breasted SF Pastel Green Gouldian Finch cock.

Red-headed White-breasted DF Pastel Green Gouldian Finch cock.

Red-headed White-breasted SF Pastel Green Gouldian Finch hen.

somewhere upon the eumelanin pathway after it diverges from the phaeomelanin pathway. White-breasted acts upon the phaeomelanin pathway, however it diverts melanin production back into the eumelanin pathway. The exact nature of this action is still unknown, however study of colour combinations of White-breasted and these other mutations can give us clues about the action of each mutation.

The Cinnamon gene acts just prior to the completion of eumelanin production. It does not reduce eumelanin production, merely altering the colour of the pigment produced. There is no interaction with the White-breasted gene and the combination is a simple summation of the effects of the two genes. In other words, a White-breasted Cinnamon colour is very close to that of the base Cinnamon mutation, merely with the breast changed to white.

The exact point of action of the Pastel gene has not been investigated by science, however we know that it is somewhere on the eumelanin pathway. Pastel removes virtually all eumelanin in homozygous (or hemizygous) form but does not reduce phaeomelanin at all. When combined with White-breasted, we discover that the White-breasted gene is diverting phaeomelanin production back into the eumelanin pathway at an earlier step to the point where Pastel has its action. As a result, the Pastel gene is able to reduce the total eumelanin produced, including the pigment that has diverted from the phaeomelanin pathway. The end result of the combination is a greater reduction of all melanin production in the bird, producing a colour closer to pure yellow in heterozygous, hemizygous and homozygous Pastel combinations. Naturally the homozygous Pastel demonstrates the greatest degree of gene function and is the yellowest bird.

In recent years, many knowledgeable breeders have interpreted the White-breasted Pastel combinations in a different way. The common belief has been that White-breasted deleted phaeomelanin and that Pastel reduced the eumelanin, with the combination merely combining these effects. However, the combination of the Australian mutation known as Dilute-backed with the White-breasted gene has shown us new aspects of the White-

The series of photographs, on this and the opposite page, illustrate how White-breasted Pastel combinations show complementary action that results in progressive loss of all melanin types.

Black-headed White-breasted SF Pastel Green Gouldian Finch cock.

Black-headed White-breasted DF Pastel Green Gouldain Finch cock.

Black-headed White-breasted SF Pastel Green Gouldian Finch hen.

Yellow-headed White-breasted SF Pastel Green Gouldian Finch cock.

Yellow-headed White-breasted DF Pastel Green Gouldian Finch cock.

Yellow-headed White-breasted SF Pastel Green Gouldian Finch hen.

Red-headed Dilute-backed Green Gouldian Finch hen.

Red-headed Dilute-backed Green split White-breasted Gouldian Finch hen.

Red-headed White-breasted Dilute-backed Green Gouldian Finch hen.

breasted gene function and demonstrated that it actually diverts phaeomelanin production into the eumelanin pathway.

The Dilute-backed mutation is similar to the Pastel mutation in that it reduces eumelanin production. However it is inheritied as autosomal recessive rather than sex-linked dominant and the eumelanin reduction falls between the Single Factor Pastel and the Double Factor Pastel phenotypes. The really interesting and surprising thing about this gene is how it interacts with the White-breasted mutation. Instead of the combined phenotype having less melanin in the plumage, overall it actually has an increase of eumelanin, which is particularly noticeable in the back areas of the plumage such as the pencil lines and bib of the Red-headed (or Yellow-headed) birds and the entire head of the Black-headed White-breasted Dilute-backed Gouldian Finch.

Black plumage in the basic Dilute-backed Gouldian Finch is reduced to less than 50% of normal production. However in the White-breasted Dilute-backed combination, the black eumelanin production is increased to levels close to those in the wildtype, at least 85% of Normal. And the other extremely interesting observation is that a Dilute-backed split for White-breasted produces black pigmentation somewhere between those two levels. The White-breasted Dilute-backed combination clearly demonstrates that the White-breasted gene diverts phaeomelanin production back into the eumelanin pathway and that the Dilute-backed gene acts somewhere close to where this happens. In addition, it shows us that the function of the recessive White-breasted locus is dose dependant. In other words, a hidden White-breasted gene in a heterozygous wildtype phenotype (Normal split White-breasted bird) is still functioning, even though that function is not normally visible.

This new information about the White-breasted gene function also serves to shed new light on other phenotypes produced by the mutation. If White-breasted merely blocked phaeomelanin, then you would expect the White-breasted Normal to have reduced body and head colour changes as these areas carry phaeomelanin, even if

The series of photographs, on this and the opposite page, illustrate how White-breasted Dilute-backed combinations show an increase in eumelanin production. Note also that Dilute-backed birds split for White-breasted have increased eumelanin as well.

Black-headed Dilute-backed Green (left) and Red-headed White-breasted Dilute-backed Green Gouldian Finch cocks.

Red-headed Dilute-backed Green split White-breasted Gouldian Finch cock.

Red-headed White-breasted Dilute-backed Green Gouldian Finch cock.

Red-headed Dilute-backed Green Gouldian Finch hen.

Red-headed Dilute-backed Green split White-breasted Gouldian Finch hen.

Red-headed White-breasted Dilute-backed Green Gouldian Finch hen.

The Lilac-breasted gene exhibits similar behaviour to the White-breasted gene when combined with either Pastel or Dilute-backed mutations.

1. Black-headed Lilac-breasted Dilute-backed Green Gouldian Finch cock.
2. & 3. Red-headed Lilac-breasted Dilute-backed Green Gouldian Finch hen.
4. Black-headed Lilac-breasted SF Pastel Green Gouldian Finch cock.
5. Black-headed Lilac-breasted DF Pastel Green Gouldian Finch cock.

only in smaller quantities than other pigments. However now that we know that the gene redirects phaeomelanin into eumelanin, we have a simple explanation of why the body colour does not visibly change in the basic White-breasted Gouldian Finch.

Taking this line of thinking further, I would suggest that perhaps Red-headed White-breasted specimens carry greater quantities of black pigment in their heads than wildtype specimens. Is this simply part of natural variation in colour for the Red-headed Normal bird or has the White-breasted gene increased eumelanin in the head by converting phaeomelanin?

Is there evidence of increased eumelanin visible in these Red-headed White-breasted Normals?

Red-headed White-breasted Green cocks (left and centre) and hen—illustrating the eumelanin conversion in the head of hens.

While discussing the White-breasted gene, we should also consider the Lilac-breasted gene which is believed to be allelic with the White-breasted mutation. If this were the case, then we would expect to see similar gene action from the Lilac-breasted mutation but to a lesser degree compared to the White-breasted gene. And in fact we do see just that, with Lilac-breasted Dilute-backed specimens showing an overall increase in eumelanin deposits and Lilac-breasted Pastel combinations exhibiting overall greater melanin reduction than the basic Pastel mutation. These observations, which are being made worldwide by different breeders, are important evidence that the Lilac-breasted is in fact a 'partial' White-breasted gene.

Considered in their entirety, the White-breasted combinations are an excellent example of what can be learnt from studying colour morphs and gene combinations. Each new combination potentially tells us a little more about gene function and pigmentation.

Red-headed Lilac-breasted SF Pastel Blue Gouldian Finch hen. (In the collection of Ray and Wendy Lowe.)

Halfsiders

There are well-documented specimens of Gouldian Finches that show plumage features of both the cock and the hen, often in a roughly half-and-half manner. This type of colour change is generally referred to as a 'halfsider', even in instances where the change on one of the 'sides' may be only a quarter of the plumage or less.

The exact nature of these Gouldian Finches has not been determined by science. However, in Zebra Finches at least one bird that exhibited both male and female plumage was shown to be a gynandromorph. This is an individual that exhibits both male and female sexual characteristics and has the different sex chromosomes (and organs) in different parts of the body. The 'halfsider' Gouldian Finches would appear to fit this category, yet have the added difference of expressing different colour morphs on each side of the body.

This is similar to 'halfsiders' in many parrot species which are not based on male/female traits, but instead differ in the mutations they express. Many are Blue one side and Green the other. This type of halfsider has nothing to do with the sex chromosomes, but a different pair of chromosomes. Some authors have suggested that they are chimeras—organisms that carry genes from two completely different sources blended together. To me, this seems unlikely, yet clearly some type of severe chromosomal damage has occurred in these birds during the early embryo stage.

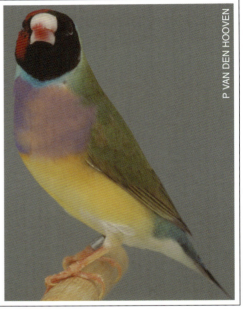

Left: Halfsider Gouldian Finch—Black-headed Normal hen (right side of bird) and Red-headed SF Pastel Green cock (left side of bird). Below: Halfsider Gouldian Finch—Red-headed Normal cock (right side of bird) and Black-headed Normal hen (left side of bird).

In the 'halfsider' Gouldian Finches illustrated here, both the sex changes and the colour morph changes relate to changes in the sex chromosomes as the affected mutations are all sex-linked. One bird can be interpreted as a Red-headed Normal split Black-headed cock that has lost the X chromosome that carried the Red-headed gene from the 'female' side of the body. Hence the Black-headed gene is expressed instead. The second bird can be interpreted as a Red-headed Single Factor Pastel Green split Black-headed cock. In this instance both the Red-headed gene and the Pastel gene were linked on one X chromosome and lost 'together', leaving only the Black-headed gene to express. If the Pastel gene were linked to the Black-headed gene on the other X chromosome, the bird would have been a Black-headed Single Factor Pastel Green hen on the second side.

'Halfsiders' may breed successfully, although they do not reproduce the 'halfsider' appearance in their offspring. Instead they breed like a bird with the (sex-linked) dominant genes split for the (sex-linked) recessive genes. The gynandromorph type 'halfsider, like the Zebra Finch specimens, generally do not breed successfully. It is yet to be confirmed if this is also the case in the Gouldian Finch specimens.

Melanism

Melanistic Gouldian Finches are well documented around the world—melanistic changes can be genetic in some instances, with a number of melanistic mutations established in Zebra Finches and some parrot species. However acquired melanism is far more common in finch species.

Acquired melanism is not a genetic change and therefore cannot be referred to as a mutation. In addition, it cannot be passed on to the next generation. The exact mechanism that brings about melanism in finches has not been studied scientifically to my knowledge; however the circumstances that bring about the changes are well documented by aviculturists. If a finch is allowed to moult while housed in environmental conditions that are too dark, melanism develops whereby varying degrees of the plumage deposit excessive melanin pigments as the feathers grow. If the housing conditions are improved, then the bird will produce normal plumage at the next moult. Whether lack of sunlight is the critical factor is not known, but the condition can be common in birds housed in dark birdrooms and also in those housed indoors in pet stores or similar.

For the finch breeder, melanism can be a difficult thing to 'pass up'. We know from Zebra Finches that true genetic melanistic mutations can occur. Zebra Finches actually have 4–5 different melanistic genes established! Yet most of the melanistic birds we find will be those with acquired melanism rather than true melanistic mutations. One day, a breeder will reject a bird as 'valueless' that will be a real 'Black' Gouldian Finch. So keep looking, but do not get your hopes too high for at least a year or two after you find the bird.

Left and above: Melanistic Gouldian Finches.

Red-headed Melanistic Green Gouldian Finch cock.

Yellow-headed Melanistic Green Gouldian Finch cock.

Extinct mutations of the Gouldian Finch.

During the 1970s, USA breeder Herschell Fry began to establish a colour morph of the Gouldian Finch that he called 'Sky Blue-breasted'. Although he produced approximately 30 cocks, he did not succeed in producing a hen and eventually the mutation died out. These are distinctly different from the occassional Blue-breasted birds sometimes produced elsewhere and discussed in this book.

A Lutino Gouldian Finch was being established in Sydney in the 1940s, with significant numbers being bred. Unfortunately the mutation became extinct after all specimens were stolen. This bird appears to be a different strain from the Lutino Gouldian Finches being bred in other regions of the world today.

GLOSSARY OF TERMS

The following is a brief glossary of a few of the technical terms used within the text on colour mutations.

Allele—an alternative gene for a particular locus. If a locus has not mutated, then it is occupied by its wildtype gene. However once mutation has occurred, it is normal to refer to all possible genes for that location as alleles for that locus, ie the wildtype allele and its alternate alleles (the mutant ones).

Autosomal—refers to the autosomes, which are all the chromosomes other than the sex chromosomes. Therefore an autosomal mutation is a mutation of a locus lying upon one of the many autosomes.

Chromosome—a chain of DNA (Deoxyribonucleic Acid). Sections of the DNA sequences form what we call genes. So the chromosome can be viewed as a chain of genes. Different species have different numbers of chromosomes, but in all cases there are two copies of each chromosome except for the sex chromosomes. The male bird has two X chromosomes forming a pair, but the female bird has only one X chromosome. The second chromosome in this pair is the Y chromosome. In birds, because the sex chromosomes are the reverse of those in mammals, the correct designation for them is, in fact, Z (for the X) and W (for the Y). However, as this designation is rarely used in aviculture, I have not used it in this book.

Co-dominant—In this form of inheritance, both alleles (the wildtype and the mutant) express themselves equally. As a result, three different phenotypes occur in this situation; the homozygous wildtype phenotype, the heterozygous phenotype and the homozygous mutant phenotype. It is also know as ***incomplete dominance***.

Colour morph—the correct term for all mutant phenotypes. The word 'morph' indicates a change; therefore colour morphs are alternate plumage colourations.

Dominant—a dominant allele is one that will express itself fully whether heterozygous or homozygous without any difference in phenotype in either situation. Dominant alleles can be either sex-linked or autosomal.

Eumelanin—a type of pigment that is naturally black in colour. It is deposited within feathers and other body parts by specialised cells called melanocytes. It is produced by the body from proteins via a chemical pathway. It may also appear as shades of grey depending on the quantity of pigment deposited and where within the feather it lies. When it is found in the outer cortex, it appears as its natural black colour. However, when it lies deeper in the medulla it appears grey. And when combined with the cloudy cell structure, it produces the blue distortion effect.

Gene—the base unit of instruction within the chromosome. Each gene codes for a specific protein that has a specific action. Each gene has a unique function and only occurs at a specific locus.

Genotype—the correct term for the genetic make-up of an organism.

Heterozygous—refers to a bird that has two different alleles for a particular locus. This could be one wildtype allele and one mutant allele, or two different mutant alleles.

Homozygous—refers to whether a bird has two identical alleles for a particular locus. The bird could have two wildtype alleles, or alternatively it could have two mutant alleles. However in both cases, the alleles the bird has to choose from are identical.

Locus (plural *loci*)—refers to the location or address where a particular gene occurs on a chromosome. Each gene has an exact locus that cannot be altered except through rare mutations. If a gene is moved from its locus, it will generally no longer function correctly.

Melanocyte, melanoblast—The melanocyte is the cell responsible for producing melanin pigment. Immature cells begin life in the neural crest of the embryo and are known as melanoblasts. They migrate throughout the skin and into other specialised areas such as the eye. Once at their final destination, they mature and differentiate into mature melanocytes. Melanocytes are not present in feathers, only skin and feather follicles. They produce particles of melanin pigment known as melanosomes, which are then transferred into the feathers.

Multiple alleles—The term used when more than one mutant allele is known to exist. As multiple alleles occupy only a single locus, the bird may carry a maximum of only two of these alleles at any one time. This has relevance when understanding the outcome of combining mutations that are multiple alleles of one another. In these cases, wildtype alleles are excluded by the presence of different mutant alleles occupying the locus on each chromosome of the pair. Therefore, without the presence of a wildtype gene, normally recessive mutations appear to behave in a dominant fashion. In Gouldian Finches, Lilac-breasted and White-breasted are alleles and it is expected that Seagreen, Turquoise and Blue will also form an allelic series.

Normal—refers to the bird in its basic colour form. Many breeders refer to the Normal bird as Purple-breasted Green, however the addition of the word 'Purple-breasted' is superfluous as this is a standard feature of all Normals. Instead, the Normal bird can simply be referred to as Green.

Phaeomelanin—a chestnut-red coloured melanin pigment. It is scattered in small quantities throughout the plumage of the Gouldian Finch. However it is concentrated in greatest levels in the breast region where the cloudy cell structure makes it appear purple.

Phenotype—refers to the physical appearance of the bird. Many different genotypes may have the same phenotype. For instance a Normal bird has a Normal phenotype but may be carrying various hidden alleles within its genotype.

Recessive—refers to the form of genetic inheritance behaviour exhibited by a mutant allele. It implies that the mutant allele is not expressed when heterozygous with the wildtype allele. By strict definition a recessive mutation can be either autosomal or sex-linked.

Wildtype allele—the Normal gene for the particular locus being discussed.

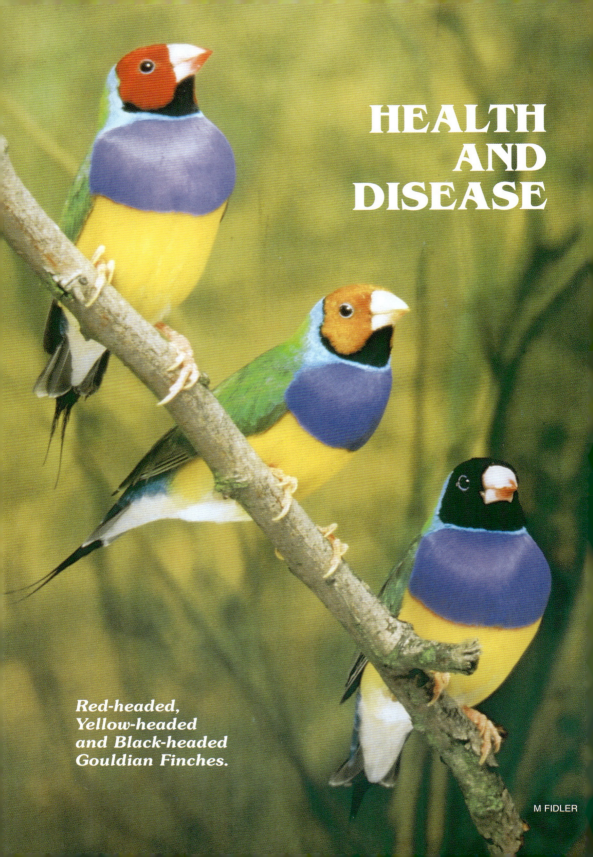

HEALTH AND DISEASE

Red-headed, Yellow-headed and Black-headed Gouldian Finches.

M FIDLER

Introduction

There is so much for us to learn about the Gouldian Finch and what they need to be happy, healthy and productive in captivity. The importance of Gouldian Finch happiness and good health as a means of ensuring breeding success is discussed in detail in the following pages.

A 'drug-free' approach to Gouldian Finch rearing is a desirable goal which can be achieved if the birds' needs are catered for and there is a strong level of gene-based immunity present in the flock. At times medicines may be required to prevent the illnesses and deaths that occur as the result of poor management practices or weak genes. The ideas and suggestions outlined here should help enthusiasts develop strong families of Normal or mutation Gouldian Finches.

Health and Happiness in the Gouldian Finch

It takes some time to understand the needs of the Gouldian Finch. Mistakes may be made in the management of Normal birds without ill effect because they are hardy and adaptable creatures. Consequences of the mistakes often go unnoticed. There is, however, far less room for mistakes when keeping and breeding the much weaker mutations. Knowledge of what makes these birds happy helps provide mutations with exactly what is needed to help them breed.

Essentials of Gouldian happiness:

- Good health regimes including regular worming, lice and mite control.
- Balanced nutrition.
- Clean food and water.
- Hygienic housing.
- Housing with own kind.
- Avoidance of overcrowding.
- Direct sunshine.
- Protection from cold and moist conditions.
- A defined breeding season similar to that experienced in nature.
- Understanding 'breeding condition' and its effect on breeding success.
- Allocation of a set time for the moult.
- No breeding when it is too cold.
- Privacy.

There is little to support the opinion that Gouldian Finches are more fragile than other finches. Normal birds are strong and should breed well in outdoor aviaries.

Overcrowding causes stress which triggers disease. Avoid housing your birds in overcrowded conditions.

However, they are different from other finches and do require special care. Knowledge of their breeding cycle and the conditions that make them happy help to make them easier to keep and breed.

Some mutations may be weak and susceptible to breeding failure and illness. They must be bred under artificial conditions and receive additional care until, as an established mutation, they are strong enough to breed outdoors.

Natural Behaviour and Health

Gouldian Finches are shy within their natural habitat and are the last finches to come to water usually in the morning and the evening. In line with their retiring personality, breeding results improve when they are housed with their own kind and are not disturbed.

Cocks and hens are protective of their nests and need space for undisturbed breeding. Aggressive behaviour is a sign of dominance, vitality, fertility and good health. Assertive behaviour may be seen in these finches from a young age and it is wise to select the most assertive youngsters (those at the top of the pecking order) when seeking to improve the overall health and reproductive capacity of mutation or Normal flocks. It may be necessary to remove over-aggressive cocks or hens as some Gouldian Finches will fight to the death.

Open-style aviaries are suitable and recommended for established and vital families of Gouldian Finches in warm climates. They are not suitable for breeding weak strains of mutations, as the conditions are often too harsh for these weaker birds. At the beginning of the breeding season, when more than two first-time mutation breeding pairs are housed together, surveillance becomes necessary. This may help to identify problem pairs that may fight excessively while competing for breeding sites—a possible cause of subsequent breeding failures.

Knowledge of the demeanour and personality of Gouldian Finches can be used as a gauge to monitor the earliest signs of ill health. The sudden onset of nervousness in otherwise calm Gouldian Finches is a reliable sign of an imminent health problem.

The correct method of restraining a finch.

General Susceptibility to Disease

In the wild, Gouldian Finches are more tolerant of less than perfect breeding conditions because they are inherently stronger and more adaptable than captive birds. The further removed captive Gouldian Finches are from nature the less adaptable and more fastidious they become. Gouldian Finches kept in dry, sheltered, outdoor or ornamental aviaries may be stronger, having adapted to conditions closer to their wild environment.

Different levels of care are required for each 'type' of Gouldian Finch, with mutations requiring the most care. Additional nutrients, as well as a more controlled environment, are required to help these fragile coloured birds to breed. Mutations are also more susceptible to cold stress than Normal birds.

First-time breeding pairs are more susceptible to problems than established breeding pairs. Cocks are especially prone to illness at the beginning of the breeding cycle. First-time breeders and weak cocks are most susceptible to disease at this time, especially bacterial diseases like *Streptococcus*. First-time hens must also endure energy-sapping physical activities of egg production and laying. It is during this stage of their breeding cycle, if the environmental and nutritional requirements are not met, that disease is more prevalent.

The problems encountered in first-time breeding pairs are lessened considerably when a nutritional health program is introduced when they are juveniles and especially during the moult and prior to the breeding season. A stringent selection and culling policy should be adopted. Birds that are first to complete the juvenile moult are the strongest and should be the first chosen for breeding.

Critical Periods for Gouldian Health

The increased incidence of disease at certain times may be explained by a disturbance of the natural cycles of Gouldian Finches and the existence of overlapping stresses. Problems are more likely to occur during critical physiological stages of young and adult birds. They remain most vulnerable to health problems at the following life stages.

Nestlings

At hatching–3 days of age

Hatching requires a substantial effort.

At two weeks of age

Gouldian Finch parents no longer brood their young from 12 days of age. Nestlings of this age cannot generate enough heat to survive the cold on their own. They huddle together to decrease their surface area and keep each other warm. However, it is impossible to maintain their body heat when ambient temperatures drop too low.

At 3–4 weeks of age

Gouldian Finches fledge at between 24–26 days of age. At this time they leave the safety and warmth of the nest. This represents a significant psychological disturbance to weaker young.

Juveniles

At 6–12 weeks of age

At six weeks of age the luminous gape spots disappear from the angle of beak when young birds wean and become self-sufficient. Their parents are also beginning to prepare for their next brood at this time. The combination of independence, parent aggression and the start of the juvenile moult exposes weak birds to illness. This is an age where adverse weather conditions have a marked affect on the health of the finches, because such large amounts of energy resources are needed to complete the juvenile moult.

Breeding Birds

Cock

Cocks are most susceptible to the effects of bad weather when they begin their energetic courtship displays. At this time the androgen (male sex) hormones are released into the bloodstream and weaken the immune system,

The first sign of disease in 3–5-day-old nestlings is red skin (dehydration) and retarded growth. Appropriate medication at this time will save this nest.

Juvenile Gouldians are highly susceptible to illness during the weaning process. Symptoms of weakness (wing drop, dull eyes and extended neck) may appear suddenly. Immediate first aid treatment is necessary to save seriously ill birds.

rendering the cocks more susceptible to illness. Weaker cocks are less able to generate their own heat and fluff their plumage out in an effort to insulate their bodies from the cold. Prolonged effort at conserving their own body heat during cold spells weakens them further. They may eat less and within days they may be too weak to eat and may subsequently die.

Hen

Hens are at risk during the exertion of producing and laying their eggs. They are at most risk of illness when laying their second clutch of eggs while still feeding young from the previous clutch. A hen becomes most susceptible after she has selected her nest and mated with her cock. She must expend enormous amounts of energy producing eggs. The hot temperatures of her natural environment preserve her energy levels, whereas in an open aviary, cold, fluctuating and wet weather may drain these energy reserves, causing egg binding and disease in the breeding hen.

Identifying Weak Individuals

Established breeding pairs rarely encounter contagious illnesses, because their health status and breeding prowess have already been tested or proven during adolescence and as first-time breeders. The majority of problems appear in weaker or older individuals that are unable to cope with the effort required to breed. As part of the continuing selection process, culling is the best option for weak birds. Enthusiasts, however, must also be able to recognise the different personalities of members within their flock in order to prevent the unnecessary removal of robust productive birds that may fall ill because of poor care and aviary conditions.

Malocclusion of the beak (cross beak) in this juvenile is most likely a congenital abnormality possibly caused by inbreeding.

Cock

Cocks that fluff up and become listless soon after breeding, when conditions are not particularly hot, should be regarded as weaklings until proven otherwise. First-time cocks, however, should be given a second chance, as most will perform satisfactorily when held back for the next breeding season. Young cocks are more likely to 'drop out' of breeding condition more often and should be held back from breeding until they have completed their next moult. They must be culled from breeding if they 'fail' in subsequent breeding seasons.

Hen

Hens should breed successfully after the completion of the first annual moult. Such hens are judged strong hens because they do not experience androgenic immunosuppression. Weak hens should not be used for future breeding. First-time hens that fall ill during egg production must be considered weaklings and are best removed from the breeding program.

DISEASE PREVENTION

Disease prevention should be an ongoing process to protect your Gouldians from illness and ensure good breeding results. These prevention measures should include regular control of mites and lice, worming and treatment for Coccidiosis.

Control of Mites and Lice

Mites and lice cause intense irritation preventing the birds, especially feeding parents, from the rest they require to remain healthy. Sick parents, rejection of young and dead chicks are common complaints associated with mite and lice infestations. Red Mite is a serious and deadly blood-sucking mite that must be controlled during the warm months of spring, summer and autumn.

Ivermectin or moxidectin-type products should be administered each month during breeding. During the warmer months, these may be added to the drinking water for two consecutive days, concurrently with the application of an insecticidal spray, eg Coopex™, into the nest and aviary.

Ivermectin and moxidectin have a dual action of killing Air Sac Mites as well as feather mites and lice.

Worming

Internal parasites are a common cause of poor development and illness in juvenile and adult birds. Worming treatments that kill worms should be administered each month during the warmer months.

Treatments to control spiders, ants, cockroaches, moths and other insects that transmit and carry tapeworms and gizzardworm are also recommended.

Coccidiosis Protection

Coccidiosis is more likely to occur whenever warm temperatures accompany rain, summer and autumn the most dangerous seasons for infection. Conditions that favour Coccidiosis may also appear during winter and spring in temperate climates.

In order to prevent Coccidiosis in the aviary, treatment should be administered for three days each month throughout the entire year.

Disease Prevention for Juvenile Gouldians

A healthy juvenile Normal Gouldian Finch.

An overcrowded aviary is not a favourable environment for the enduring health of young birds and outbreaks of disease should be anticipated. Adolescence, which spans a 4–6 month period from independence until the attainment of adult plumage, is the most critical age of captive Gouldians. To remain healthy they must be provided with special care and then given an opportunity in spring to start and complete their juvenile moult.

Normal and mutation adolescent Gouldians should be removed from breeding aviaries and placed into a 'young bird aviary' to reduce the psychological stress of overcrowding, parental aggression and the problems of adolescence. Poor housing conditions, in particular, expose juveniles to illnesses that may then contaminate the remainder of the aviary and infect breeding pairs. It is not necessary to remove young Gouldians from large colony breeding aviaries where spacious conditions resemble natural conditions. In this setting juveniles from successive nests may happily coexist with their parents and help feed subsequent young.

Adolescents enjoy spending time with youngsters of a similar age and enjoy roosting together. This community type activity is an important emotional health tonic, especially for weaker mutations. It engenders a feeling of safety and wellbeing that alleviates stress and promotes natural health at this critical developmental age.

Adolescent Gouldians experience most psychological stress within the first week of entering the young bird aviary. This stress is alleviated considerably by introducing clutches of a similar age at the same time.

This Gouldian Finch is 'stuck in the moult'.

Overcrowding, competition for food, water and perch space, aggression from older, more assertive youngsters and exposure to germs are the main physical factors affecting the health of adolescents introduced to the young bird aviary. Weaker birds under stress are susceptible to illness from *E. coli*, *Streptococcus*, worms and Coccidiosis. These infections spread rapidly and eventually infect even the strongest youngsters. Germs may accumulate in high numbers in the drinking water and on the floor. Health problems are alleviated by good management practices that lessen these psychological and physical stresses.

Until they achieve full adult plumage Normal and mutation Gouldians are at considerable health risk, especially during periods of temperature extremes and high humidity. Bacterial bowel infections (predominantly *E. coli*, *Campylobacter*, *Streptococcus* infections), Ornithosis (Chlamydophila), mould (Aspergillosis), yeast (Candida) and parasitic infections (Coccidiosis, Atoxoplasmosis, *Cochlosoma*, Air Sac Mite, worms) account for most juvenile deaths. Preventative medicines should be used during this time to control these troublesome infections and to help the young birds through this difficult stage of their development.

Juvenile Gouldians should be housed together until they have 'coloured up' completely. Careful observation of adolescent mutations during this time will help to select potentially good breeding stock. Those that 'colour up' quickly are considered to be the most vital individuals and should be identified with coloured rings, and then placed together as first choice breeding stock. These strong birds should be treated in exactly the same manner as Normal Gouldians so that they develop as naturally as possible. Those that moult more slowly are potential 'weaklings' and need special care during their first breeding season. These must be housed separately from the strong birds. The selection of future breeding based upon the speed of their first moult is a most important part of improving the health and breeding performance of Gouldian mutations.

DIAGNOSIS OF DISEASES

The correct diagnosis of finch illnesses can be difficult and should be done in consultation with an avian veterinarian who has experience with finches. A complete pathology analysis is needed to diagnose a serious problem. Less serious problems can often be diagnosed over the phone or by the microscopic testing of a dropping sent by post.

Finch enthusiasts are encouraged to learn how to use a microscope to manage the health of their aviaries and to use veterinarians for additional advice. The microscope provides Gouldian keepers with an opportunity to catch an illness in the earliest stages of its development and, in doing so, helps to save sick individuals and protect the health of the flock. The purpose of learning microscopic techniques is to develop sufficient skills to identify and work with illness and disease in the quickest possible way. **Under the Microscope** by Dr Danny Brown and published by **ABK Publications** is a valuable resource. It outlines the microscopic findings of the common diseases of birds.

Dropping Analysis

Finch droppings offer a wealth of information concerning the health of a bird. Changes in the dropping indicates a potential health problem. A change in the colour and consistency of the dropping associated with a fluffed-up bird indicates a need for a microscopic examination.

Instructions for collecting dropping samples:
- Collect fresh abnormal droppings with a cotton bud.
- Place them into a sealed plastic bag or canister.
- Place contents in an envelope and send via express post to your avian veterinarian for analysis.
- Telephone the next day for the results and recommendations.

Antibiotics

Prescription antibiotics should be restricted to the treatment of sick individuals in a hospital cage. Antibiotics used in this way should help preserve the long-term health of finches housed in outdoor collections. Only under special circumstances, eg when many birds are dying during a disease outbreak, should prescription medicines be administered to protect the entire flock.

Prudent use of antibiotic medicines has been beneficial in nurturing new colour mutations. Often medical intervention is the only assistance available to ensure that birds can reproduce the genes of these weak families. Irreplaceable colour genes would have been lost without a medicinal approach to the problem of rearing many fragile mutations. Medicines used wisely will save seriously ill individual birds and help them breed. Medicines may also be used to nurture weak individuals and families into breeding condition. With great care the progeny of these weak individuals can become strong enough to breed independently without help from foster-parents or medicines. With the establishment of a good gene pool there is no longer a danger of losing the mutation and a more natural approach to maintaining the health of these mutations must then be introduced. *The short-term benefits of administering antibiotics to weak mutation Gouldian Finches must not be regarded as a long-term cure for these birds.* Overall, it is the attention to detail, strict hygiene and good management practices rather than the use of medicines that remain the best long-term solutions to strengthen and establish families of previously weak mutations.

Emergency First Aid

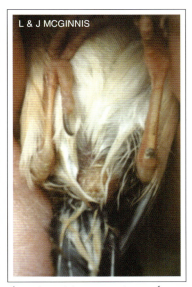

Emergency first aid for finches may be unrewarding when treatment is delayed because their high metabolic rate and small size expose them to a rapid death. No amount of treatment or intensive care will save finches showing signs of weight loss and muscle wasting—usually birds that have not eaten for 24 hours.

Early detection of any illness is necessary to obtain good treatment success rates (almost 100% cure). Therefore, sick finches must be removed to a heated hospital cage at the very first sign of sickness. The body heat of a sick bird must be quickly restored. A hospital cage heated to 28–30°C provides ideal conditions to restore the bird's normal body temperature (about 42°C) and stimulate appetite. Gouldians housed outdoors may prefer a temperature of 25°C as higher temperatures may place them under stress. Use a hot water bottle or a bar heater if there is no hospital cage.

Glucose-enriched electrolytes administered in the drinking water will help rehydrate the bird and provide it with an immediate energy source. As long as the finch is still drinking, the energy levels are quickly restored and the all important appetite returns. A bird that is not eating should receive a heated, high-energy nutrition formula, eg a high-quality handrearing formula.

A wet vent is a symptom of acute stress. Immediate removal to a heated hospital cage for first aid treatment is recommended for all birds exhibiting a wet vent.

A suitable hospital cage for housing sick birds.

After the bird starts eating, appropriate antibiotics for the symptoms displayed by the bird may then be added to the drinking water (or administered directly if the bird is not drinking) together with the glucose-enriched electrolytes.

The floor of the hospital cage should be lined with clean paper towel so that the droppings can be easily monitored and gathered for veterinary analysis. Once the illness has been diagnosed appropriate medication can be prescribed.

The hospital cage should be free of grit and sand until recovery is complete because ill birds can over-engorge on grit, obstructing the gizzard. The hospital cage should be cleaned and disinfected each day with minimal disturbance to the ill bird.

Earliest Symptoms of Illness

Tired Eyes (Lazy Eyelids)
The appearance of tired, dull eyes should warrant closer investigation.

Inactivity
Sick finches roost in the one place, usually on the feed station, to conserve energy. Often a collection of their droppings accumulates in this location. It is helpful to examine the size, consistency, colour and smell of these droppings and preferably organise a sample for veterinary diagnosis.

Change in Feather Colour
A loss of colour intensity and sheen of the feathers is a very early sign of illness.

'Pooled' faecal samples are a useful means of screening small flocks.

Fluffed-up Appearance
Sick birds eat less and fluff their feathers to conserve body heat and keep warm.

Droppings
A change in the size, consistency, colour and smell of droppings are symptoms of ill health. Enlarged droppings indicate impaired health. Watery droppings result from an increased thirst. Colour changes and an odour to droppings are often, but not always, a sign of disease.

Heavy Breathing
Fluffed-up finches may be seen to breathe heavily. Open-mouth breathing and tail bobbing are early signs of breathing difficulty. Tail bobbing may also be seen with Coccidiosis and egg binding.

Hunched Appearance
Most gastrointestinal and reproductive diseases in finches cause discomfort for the birds. This often produces a hunched appearance.

Symptoms of Cold Stress
Many finch species are susceptible to the effects of cold stress, with the weakest birds the first to show symptoms. A slightly fluffed-up appearance, a wet vent and a 'dopey' eye in a bird that is still in good feather are early signs of cold stress.

Noisy Respiration
Clicking, squeaking, coughing and muffled voice are early signs of upper and lower respiratory tract diseases.

Symptomatic Conditions and Treatments
It should be stated that it is far better to confirm a diagnosis before initiating treatment rather than to decide on a treatment based upon symptoms and probabilities. Symptomatic treatment of Gouldian illnesses, however, may become necessary for those unable to diagnose the problem using a microscope or for those who do not have access to an avian veterinarian. This section has been written with these people in mind.

Droppings
Changes in size, colour, smell and consistency of the droppings of any one bird should be viewed with caution.

Size
The size of the dropping is a very good indicator of the fitness and health of Gouldians. The metabolism of healthy, active and fit birds purrs with efficiency and requires minimal energy to run at top capacity. Gouldians in top health eat and drink less because their energy systems are highly efficient. They produce droppings that are small, tight, low in water and well formed. The fittest birds have the smallest droppings. Large droppings are produced when the birds require additional energy and eat more food.

Large droppings reflect a continuing stress, eg cold weather, wet spells and overcrowding. Birds with large droppings should be attended to immediately to prevent ongoing problems such as bowel infections.

Small droppings are signs of health and fitness. Healthy birds with small droppings are active and alert. However, small droppings may also indicate that a bird is eating less because of an illness. Such birds will be fluffed up, inactive and may be low in body condition.

Colour
A change in the colour of the droppings accompanying an increase in size is often the first visible sign of a potential health problem that must be investigated.

Green-coloured droppings may be due to a diet change to greenfoods, a bird eating less, diseases involving the liver and intestines (poisons, bacterial, fungal and protozoan infections), and the inappropriate use of medications.

Mustard-yellow-coloured droppings indicate a digestion problem. *Campylobacter* infection which produces large amounts of undigested amylum, must be considered the cause of mustard-coloured droppings in nestling, juvenile and newly acquired Gouldians. *Staphylococcus* and *Streptococcus* infection infecting the pancreas may sometimes produce pale yellow droppings in adult birds.

White or creamy-coloured droppings indicate 'urine' alone is being passed in the dropping. It is usually a sign of a seriously ill bird. Gizzard obstructions from engorging sand or grit, intestinal blockages by tapeworms and failure to eat are the most likely cause of white droppings. Birds with white droppings should receive immediate first aid treatment.

Black droppings indicate bleeding into the bowel. Starvation, Megabacteria (Avian Gastric Yeast) and tapeworm infestations are the most common causes of black droppings.

Yellow droppings are signs of severe liver disease. The remains of the 'urine' part of the dropping sometimes wet the vent feathers, leaving a bright yellow stain. Sometimes yellow-stained (from excessive bile pigments entering the circulation) vent feathers reflect a liver disease or *Cochlosoma* infection. *Cochlosoma* infection must also be considered the cause of yellow-coloured droppings in nestlings.

Bloody droppings are caused by starvation, obstructions, tapeworms, dehydration or as a side effect of the improper administration of antibiotics. Birds with bloody droppings usually die.

Brown droppings are usually a diarrhoea and relate to bacterial (*Clostridium* sp.) infection associated with poor aviary or water (*Pseudomonas* infection) hygiene, Megabacteria (Avian Gastric Yeast) infection, worms or sand/grit gizzard obstruction. An offensive odour may accompany *Pseudomonas* infections.

There are many possible causes of a pasted vent. Veterinary assistance may be required to identify the exact cause of infection.

Dirty Vent

Pasted or caked vents, ie droppings attached to feathers around the vent, indicate a long-standing and potentially serious illness that is capable of infecting the entire flock. Removal of the caked dropping often reveals a sweet, chicken-like smell that indicates a bacterial infection—usually *E. coli*, *Clostridium*, *Streptococcus* or Thrush (*Candida*). Finches with low grade Megabacteria (Avian Gastric Yeast) infections may have hard, dry black droppings caked around the vent. Finches with a Thrush (*Candida*) infection may have dark green, greasy and sweet-smelling droppings caked around the vent. Finches with uterine infections—*Streptococcus*, *Clostridium* and anaerobic infections—may have moist, large khaki-green-coloured droppings caked around the vent that carry a particularly pungent odour when removed.

Smell

E. coli, *Cochlosoma*, Thrush (*Candida*), Coccidiosis and *Yersinia* infections are causes of smelly droppings in finches. Healthy droppings carry no odour. There is a fresh, clean smell to the healthy aviary. *E. coli* and Thrush (*Candida*) infections produce a sweet, 'chicken-like' smell in an infected aviary. It is helpful to smell the droppings of sick birds.

Diarrhoea

Watery droppings occur in birds with excessive thirst. Hot days, protozoan parasites (Coccidiosis, *Cochlosoma*, *Trichomonas*), crop infections, Thrush (*Candida*) and toxic fungal infections, fevers, sugar-based vitamins or medicines produce watery droppings because of increased water intake. Stress in the aviary may also produce watery droppings. Adult 'carriers' of *Cochlosoma* may exhibit watery droppings as their only sign of infection.

Many diseases may produce diarrhoea—
- Coccidiosis produces a diarrhoea that often smells.
- *E. coli* infections may or may not produce diarrhoea.
- *Yersinia* infections causes severe diarrhoea.
- Megabacteria (Avian Gastric Yeast) infections produce a dark brown-black watery diarrhoea.
- Ornithosis (*Chlamydophila*) produces a green-coloured diarrhoea.

Undigested Seed in Droppings

Cochlosoma, Megabacteria (Avian Gastric Yeast), *Giardia* infections and Thrush (*Candida*) are common causes of large watery droppings that may also contain undigested seed. The poor absorption of nutrients weakens infected birds. They become very thin and weak. Weakness may be confused with neurological symptoms.

Cochlosoma, Megabacteria (Avian Gastric Yeast) and Thrush (*Candida*) are likely causes of this symptom in nestlings and juveniles between the ages of 10 days and six

Post-mortem specimen showing thickened gizzard lining and (undigested) whole seeds in the intestine. Further diagnostics will be needed to determine if this is due to a bacterial, fungal or parasitic disease.

weeks, during the juvenile moult, or after a cold or wet period. *Cochlosoma* infection of Gouldians occurs in association with Bengalese Finches or other 'carrier' birds. In the absence of carrier birds, Thrush (*Candida*) is the more likely cause of seeds in droppings and is more likely to occur in Gouldian mutations when there is concurrent Ornithosis (*Chlamydophila*) (check fertility), overcrowding or with poor seed sprouting technique.

Feather Loss

On the Head

This common problem may be caused by hormonal or nutritional imbalance, behavioural problems, or fungal or mite infestation. Breeding season baldness in hens may occur at the conclusion of the moult just prior to breeding condition or when breeding out of season. Birds may be hormonally confused because of artificial lighting (especially flicking neon tubes) and temperature control.

Around the Eye

This is a reliable sign of sinusitis, conjunctivitis or a corneal ulcer. Causes include bacterial, fungal, blood parasite or mite infection.

Feather loss may be attributed to nutritional, parasitic or hormonal causes.

Wing or Tail Feathers

Wing or tail feather loss is usually related to an abnormal moult or Polyomavirus infection.

Abnormal body moult is usually due to a cold spell during the moult, a nutritional deficiency or disease—especially Thrush (*Candida*) and *Cochlosoma* infections in juvenile Gouldians.

Feet Problems

Feet problems are extremely stressful for birds. Swelling of toes or feet may be associated with mosquito bites, nesting material caught around the toe, injury or ergot poisoning (caused by eating grass infected with fungus). Lameness in Gouldian Finches is usually related to injury.

Examination of the wing will show if the moult is complete. The primary flight feathers are the last to moult.

Polyomavirus infection is the most likely cause of an overgrown beak in juvenile Gouldians.

Beak Abnormalities

A deformed or long beak in juvenile Gouldian Finches is a sign of Polyomavirus. Such birds should not be used for breeding. A pale colour of the beak may indicate a vitamin deficiency, blood parasites or Polyomavirus.

Beak Scratching

Scratching or rubbing the beak on the perch may be a normal activity in the Gouldian. Excessive beak rubbing or head shaking indicates sinus (Air Sac Mite, *Mycoplasma*, fungal) or mouth (Thrush) infections. Vitamin A deficiency may also be involved.

Eye Symptoms

Discharge of the eye is usually accompanied by rubbing of the face on the perch, signalling conjunctivitis. Conjunctivitis has many causes including Ornithosis (*Chlamydophila*), a generalised bacterial infection (*E. coli* or *Streptococcus*), a blood parasite, vitamin deficiency or excess, or an injury/ulcer when only one eye is infected. Birds with an *E. coli* infection demonstrate a general malaise, with or without diarrhoea. Some birds may also have a nasal discharge (rhinitis). Some birds may die. *Streptococcus* infections may show as sneezing or coughing.

This bird has a 'one-eye cold', a sinus infection that affects one eye, causing conjunctivitis. Chlamydophila, Mycoplasma, Streptococcal and fungal infections are possible causes of this condition.

Breathing Difficulties

Breathing difficulties involving open-mouth breathing with a clicking sound usually indicate Air Sac Mite infestation. Birds infested with these mites have bouts of normal activity. The mortality rate is low.

Blood-sucking mites (Red Mite) also cause minor to severe respiratory symptoms with anaemia and sometimes a high mortality. Severe depression and inactivity are consistently observed.

Coughing or Sneezing

Coughing, sneezing and gurgling sounds when breathing may also be noticed in birds with bacterial and Thrush (*Candida*) infections of the throat. These birds will be very fluffed up and inactive. Coughing or sneezing may also indicate a fungal or bacterial sinus infection. Birds with this type of infection are usually alert and active. Coughing and wheezing are also symptoms of *Streptococcus* infection.

Respiratory Symptoms and Deaths

Yersinia infections and poisoning produce many deaths within a short period, eg between hatching and three weeks of age. Other symptoms include diarrhoea. *Salmonella* causes symptoms similar to a *Yersinia* infection but deaths occur over a longer period. Ornithosis (*Chlamydophila*) elicits respiratory and eye symptoms with few deaths over a long period of time and usually after inclement weather.

Respiratory Symptoms Associated with Vomiting

Trichomoniasis (Canker) produces respiratory symptoms as well as regurgitation, bubble blowing and emaciation. Droppings are usually slimy and a dark green colour. Diarrhoea is seldom seen. The birds become depressed and inactive.

Respiratory Symptoms Failing to Respond to Antibiotic Treatment

Moulding Disease (Aflatoxicosis) and Cytomegalovirus are the most likely causes. Infection produces conjunctivitis and respiratory problems in Australian finches.

Going Light

The breast should be examined for signs of 'going light'.

'Going light' refers to the symptom of progressive weight loss. The bird is depleting its body reserves as a source of energy. Birds 'go light' with Coccidiosis, *E. coli*, *Yersinia*, *Salmonella* and fungal infections because these diseases affect the appetite. Diseases such as *Cochlosoma*, Megabacteria (Avian Gastric Yeast), *Giardia* infections and Thrush (*Candida*) are also common causes of 'going light'. These diseases affect the absorption of nutrients in the bowel. Undigested seeds may also be seen in the droppings of birds with these diseases. Blood parasites and bacterial infections may also cause progressive weight loss.

Vomiting

Vomiting usually indicates crop, stomach and gizzard problems or a poison of some sort. Megabacteria (Avian Gastric Yeast), Trichomoniasis (Canker) and blockages are common causes of vomiting. Birds with Megabacteria (Avian Gastric Yeast) do not show respiratory signs and may pass part or whole seeds in soft, watery and dark green to brown-black faeces. Birds with blocked gizzards are depressed and pass white droppings.

Head Twirling and Stargazing

Head twirling and stargazing are sometimes stress-induced. Nutritional imbalances (vitamin E deficiency), bright lights (especially flickering neon-type tubes) poisons, starvation, Atoxoplasmosis, Toxoplasmosis or viral infections may also cause these neurological signs. A sudden, severe onset of a Thrush (*Candida*) infection may precipitate head twirling.

Symptoms of poisoning include an obvious salivation, breathing difficulties, diarrhoea and inactivity. Symptoms of starvation include black-stained droppings or diarrhoea and a weakness that is often interpreted as neurological. Sudden death of several birds and head twirling in others are common symptoms of Paramyxovirus. Mortality rate is low while symptomatic birds continue to eat.

Atoxoplasmosis produces neurological signs, fluffed-up juvenile birds, going light, diarrhoea and death. Mortality can be as high as 80%. Toxoplasmosis produces neurological symptoms and temporary blindness. The diagnosis of most neurological diseases requires histopathology. Treatment should be withheld until the exact diagnosis has been reached.

Breeding Symptoms

Dead-in-Shell and Infertility

These symptoms relate commonly to a bacterial problem or a low level of protein in the breeding diet. Water hygiene and protein levels in the breeding diet should be reassessed. Ornithosis (*Chlamydopila*) and *Salmonella* infections are common causes of dead-in-shell chicks and infertility.

Stunted and Dying Nestlings

Deaths of nestlings at 1–3 days of age occur because of *E. coli* or *Campylobacter* infections, poor incubation by parents due to disease, cold weather or a nutritional problem.

Deaths of chicks from pin-feather age to fledging may be related to *Cochlosoma*, *Campylobacter*, *E. coli* or Thrush (*Candida*) infections, poor incubation by parents due to disease (eg Ornithosis), cold weather or a nutritional problem.

E. coli infections produce wet, smelly nests (stained yellow by the diarrhoea of the nestlings) and sticky wet feathers. Most deaths occur between 1–3 days of age. A chicken-like smell usually accompanies *E. coli* infections.

Campylobacter infections produce very high losses of nestlings from a young age. Infected juveniles and adults show mustard-yellow-coloured diarrhoea.

Thrush (*Candida*) infections produce stunted nestlings. The crop bloats with air and a thickened crop wall is relatively common. In fledglings and adult birds, diarrhoea and moult problems are more prominent.

Cochlosoma infections affect nestlings from 10 days to six weeks of age. Fledglings are poor quality and have yellow diarrhoea. Juveniles experience difficulties during the moult. Seeds may be seen in the droppings.

Sick and Dying Juveniles

Coccidiosis usually affects one finch species at a time, attacking the weakest birds first. Deaths are common.

E. coli infections can be a high cause of mortality in juveniles during the moult when wet and cold weather lowers their resistance to disease.

Campylobacter infections in fledglings can lead to a fluffed-up appearance, poor moult, yellow droppings and high mortality. Adult birds are carriers.

Thrush (*Candida*) infections produce very sick and dying finches. Infection in juveniles is often related to poor nutrition, crowded conditions, wet, cold spells, food spoilage and the uncontrolled use of antibiotics. A sweet smell accompanies watery droppings. Whole seeds may be seen in the droppings.

Cochlosoma infections affect finches up to three months of age. Sickness and death may occur. Juveniles experience difficulties during the moult. Seeds may be seen in mustard-coloured droppings.

Incorrect feeding of breeding Gouldian Finches may result in poor feather development in their young. Megabacteria infection may also cause malnutrition and poor feathering in juvenile Gouldian Finches.

Trichomoniasis (Canker) commonly infects juvenile finches. Infected juveniles become very depressed, go light, have moult problems and may also show respiratory symptoms.

Ornithosis (*Chlamydophila*) produces recurrent (eye and nostril) respiratory infections.

Nutritional problems are common causes of secondary bacterial infections.

Polyomavirus is a major cause of secondary infections in Gouldian mutations. Fluffed-up, listless juvenile mutations are likely to have Polyomavirus especially if they grow long beaks. Streptococcal infections are usually secondary to Polyomavirus infections in mutations. Symptoms of Streptococcal infections during the breeding season are indistinguishable from those of Ornithosis (*Chlamydophila*).

DISEASES AND DISORDERS

Aspergillosis

The inhaled and ingested forms of Aspergillosis may occur together or alone. The inhaled form of Aspergillosis is relatively uncommon in Gouldian Finches considering the cultivated nature of most outdoor finch aviaries. Juveniles are susceptible during the moult while feeding parents are susceptible during or soon after wet spells. A moist environment with poor ventilation predisposes finches to the inhaled form of Aspergillosis. Infection occurs when birds inhale fungal spores present in the nest or the aviary. The inhaled spores may accumulate in the air sac, forming abscesses.

Symptoms

- Gasping.
- Open-mouth breathing.
- Clicking respiration followed by rapid death.
- Weight loss.
- Juvenile deaths during the moult.
- Neurological symptoms of head twirling, stargazing and dizziness.

Treatment

Individuals do not usually respond to treatment.

Moulding Disease (Aflatoxicosis)

The ingestion of mouldy food contaminated with fungal toxins causes the more common ingested form of Aspergillosis (Moulding Disease or Aflatoxicosis). I refer to this disease as 'Moulding Disease' as food moulds other than *Aspergillus* may also produce toxins that are harmful to Gouldians.

Mould-affected food has a lower nutritional value than clean food and is capable of producing poisonous toxins. Many of these toxins can affect the health and breeding performance of infected birds. The toxins can ultimately harm the immune system, causing other diseases in susceptible finches. The presence of mould in the aviary or on the droppings, associated with recurrent illness and soft-shelled eggs, strongly suggests Moulding Disease.

For the best breeding performance, finches must eat food that is free of mould or mould toxins.

I believe that Moulding Disease, together with Ornithosis (*Chlamydophia*) and overcrowding, is the most important cause of disease in Gouldian aviaries. Moulting juveniles, juveniles in an overcrowded aviary and genetically weakened Gouldian mutations are the most susceptible. Gouldian mutations housed indoors are often fragile and have a weak constitution. It is not surprising, therefore, that they are the first to be affected by Moulding Disease, a disease repelled by most strong and healthy birds.

The primary factors involved in the disease are immune suppression, weak genes (in mutations), malnutrition, and a contaminated environment. Softfoods, soaked, decaying seeds left in an aviary and unhygienically prepared foods are common sources of Moulding Disease. Therefore the first objective in preventing this disease is to ensure that only clean, dry seed and hygienically prepared softfoods and soaked seed are fed to your birds.

Symptoms

There is an obvious change in the health of the aviary within a week of feeding contaminated food. The signs of Moulding Disease resemble those seen with Megabacteria (Avian Gastric Yeast) and Coccidiosis.

- The birds are quiet with little activity and show signs of 'going light'. Many birds are fluffed up, hunched, ill and sit on the floor near seed containers. Such birds often 'go light'.

- Droppings are often large and dark green and consistently poor. These are slimy with a copious quantity of green staining urate.
- Moulding Disease weakens the immune system, predisposing finches to infections that under normal circumstances they would repel. A weakened immunity caused by Moulding Disease should be considered in aviaries with recurrent illnesses caused by *Cochlosoma, Campylobacter*, Ornithosis (*Chlamydophila*), *E. coli* or *Trichomonas* infections.
- The presence of mould on the droppings on the aviary floor is the most obvious sign of Moulding Disease, but it is important for the fancier to look very carefully at the mould.
- The birds engorge on grit, because of the vitamin and mineral deficiencies that accompany the disease. Vomiting may occur, due to a blocked gizzard.

Treatment
There is no treatment for this disorder although mildly affected birds may recover.

Campylobacter Infection

Campylobacter fetus jejuni is commonly identified in the intestines of Gouldian Finches. The most common cause is stress from overcrowding, poor nutrition and weak genes. Adult birds are carriers, transmitting the disease to their young. An important part of prevention is the identification of these 'carrier' birds. The disease is linked to weak families of Gouldians that require additional energy and nutritional requirements to breed successfully. Gouldian mutations bred in small cages or in box-type aviaries are especially susceptible. *Campylobacter* infection is far more common when Bengalese Finches are used as foster-parents. Gouldian Finches housed outdoors are less likely to become infected. The disease causes voluminous solid droppings due to large amounts of undigested amylum. Infected adults eat well but fail to thrive.

Symptoms
Nestlings
- High mortality rate with yellow droppings.

Fledglings
- Inactivity and lethargy.
- Delayed moult and other moult abnormalities.
- Yellow diarrhoea or yellow, solid popcorn-like droppings.
- Weight loss.
- High mortality rate.

Adults
- Apathy and lack of vitality.
- Moult abnormalities.
- Voluminous yellow diarrhoea or solid popcorn-like droppings.
- Weight loss.

Treatment
Repeat doses of erythromycin administered during the breeding season may help establish Gouldian mutations but perpetuate weak, future generations and do little to prevent the recurrence of *Campylobacter* infection. The administration of erythromycin on a regular basis to prevent juvenile and nestling deaths may be necessary and justified while establishing weak mutations or when Bengalese Finches are used as foster-parents.

Erythromycin may be used to treat individual Gouldian Finches during their juvenile moult. A three-day treatment each month should be adequate to protect the birds until they 'colour up'. After the completion of the juvenile moult the immune system should be developed enough to repel infections naturally. Erythromycin should not be administered to 'fully coloured' Gouldians as a preventative medicine. Erythromycin is a prescription medication and cannot, therefore, be purchased without consultation with your avian veterinarian.

Coccidiosis

Coccidiosis is a disease of wet conditions, dirt-floored aviaries, fluctuating temperatures, another disease, poor nutrition or where young birds are weakened by poor genes. Coccidiosis is rarely a problem when the floor of the aviary is kept dry. Finches housed in outdoor aviaries are at most risk because it is impossible to keep floors dry during wet conditions. The disease remains a problem for indoor cages and box-type aviaries when leaking or spilt drinkers wet the floors of the cage or feed stations. However, dry aviary conditions do not always preclude the presence of Coccidiosis because outbreaks may appear secondary to other diseases.

Coccidiosis is a common and often fatal disease of finches, impairing the absorption of nutrients from the bowel. The disease lessens breeding opportunities because it weakens feeding parents, preventing them from feeding their young optimally.

Weaning and adolescent finches are vulnerable to Coccidiosis because they have not yet developed immunity to this illness, which can suddenly affect juvenile finches soon after a change in weather conditions. The most likely seasons for an outbreak are summer (after rain) and autumn (with increasing humidity) when the aviaries are crowded with young birds. Young finches are the first to die during an outbreak.

Juvenile Blue mutations housed outdoors are particularly susceptible to Coccidiosis within three weeks after fledging. Typical signs of acute death include a wet, stained vent, black bowel seen through the abdomen and minimal wasting of the pectoral mass. Health programs using Coccidiosis treatments for three days within a month after fledging and repeated every five weeks will prevent unnecessary losses.

Symptoms

- Watery droppings.
- Severe depression.
- Fluffed-up appearance.
- Shaking.
- Weight loss followed by dark green, tacky, smelly diarrhoea.

These symptoms should start to disappear after three days of treatment.

Treatment

The control of Coccidiosis in finches is aided by creating dry conditions. Diatomaceous earth is ideally suited to earthen-floored aviaries and can play an important part in the prevention of Coccidiosis. It is used to dry the aviary floors during prolonged wet spells and slows the spread of this disease.

At the same time Baycox™ (toltrazuril 25g) should be added to the drinking water of the rest of the flock. New coccidiocides (eg Baycox™) have been found to be more effective and palatable for finches than the older coccidiostats (eg Amprolium™). Baycox™ administered at low doses makes it perfectly safe for parents feeding young nestlings.

E. coli Infection

E. coli and other intestinal bacteria (eg *Enterobacter* spp., *Klebsiella* spp. and *Citrobacter* spp.) are common in outdoor aviaries and are a frequent cause of high mortality. They may cause enteritis, septicaemia (blood poisoning) and death in finches of any age and sex. Under most conditions, water cleansers should provide outdoor aviaries with good protection but at times they are not enough to prevent infection and death.

These infections often result from poor aviary conditions. Open-air aviaries with earthen floors create a perfect environment for *E. coli* infections after rain. Soaked seed, decaying food remnants, spilled water from water displays and fountains also create the moisture favoured by *E. coli*. The bacteria may also be introduced into the aviary by a 'carrier' bird, mice, rodents or insects such as cockroaches. *E. coli* infections are often associated with other concurrent diseases, notably Ornithosis (*Chlamydophila*), fungal and Polyomavirus infections. Temperature and humidity also play an important part in the onset of this disease.

Symptoms
- Lethargy.
- Large, watery green droppings.

Treatment

Sulfadiazine/trimethoprim combination antibiotics have a wide spectrum of activity and may be used as the first line of attack when birds are housed in outdoor aviaries.

The use of these antibiotics should be restricted to sick individuals who have been removed from the flock into a warmed hospital cage for treatment. The antibiotics must be administered in the drinking water when deadly outbreaks occur. They should not be administered to flocks housed in outdoor aviaries when birds are sick but not dying. Instead, the aviary should be cleaned and strong water cleansers added to the aviary drinking water.

Megabacteria Infection (Avian Gastric Yeast)

This disease occurs most commonly in Gouldian mutations and rarely in Normals from which it can be deduced that the disease reflects a poor genetic background and a depressed level of natural resistance to the disease, rather than Megabacteria itself being a particularly nasty germ. Megabacteria is an opportunistic germ, having no harmful effect upon strong vital birds. It causes illness and death in birds with a weakened immune system.

Megabacteria (Avian Gastric Yeast) is most often a secondary disease similar in nature to and managed in the same way as Trichomoniasis (Canker), Thrush (*Candida*) and Streptococcal infections. Infected birds fail to thrive and become unwell during times of stress, notably during fledging, the juvenile moult and soon after pairing. Most birds in the aviary remain healthy during an apparent outbreak unless there is another disease present or the management is poor. The first birds to become ill during a Megabacteria (Avian Gastric Yeast) outbreak in the aviary are invariably related (genetically linked). These susceptible families can be easily identified during the early stages of an outbreak and the 'carrier' parent birds eliminated from further breeding. Megabacteria (Avian Gastric Yeast) infection in the aviary occurs mostly after the 'carrier' birds experience a stressful episode, such as a show. Healthy young birds become infected under the stress of overcrowding or other diseases.

Symptoms
- Increased appetite.
- Weakness and metabolic disturbances.
- Going light.
- Fluffed-up appearance.
- Trembling.
- Hunching forward.
- Sitting on the feed dish or the ground appearing to eat and vomit.
- Undigested seed found in droppings.
- Very ill birds may exhibit bizarre behaviour consistent with central nervous system (brain) disturbances, eg walking in circles, stargazing, vomiting, muscle twitching, lack of coordination during flight (backwards, upside down), and fainting attacks.
- Hens may be egg bound, lay soft-shelled eggs or become paralysed after laying their eggs.

Birds with Megabacteria (Avian Gastric Yeast) may survive for a long time. Infected birds are more likely to die during a cold spell. Low-grade infection in birds may appear as a hunched (due to stomach pain), fluffed-up appearance.

Megabacteria (Avian Gastric Yeast) damages the glands so that the digestive juices are not produced. The symptoms occur because the Megabacteria (Avian Gastric Yeast) damages the digestive capacity of the stomach organs (proventriculus, isthmus and gizzard). In healthy finches, these organs produce acids, enzymes, mucous and other glandular secretions, which together with the grinding action of the gizzard are essential for the digestion of the food. Infected canaries virtually starve to death because none of the energy or nutrients from the food eaten is digested or absorbed into the body. The result is a constantly hungry bird that fails to gain weight, becomes very weak and may eventually die from starvation or from another illness. Finches are more susceptible to the effects of hypoglycemia (low blood glucose) and bizarre neurological signs including hypoglycaemic fits, fainting and coma because of their high metabolic rate and small size.

Megabacteria (Avian Gastric Yeast) is diagnosed easily by the microscopic testing of the droppings or by the examination of the organs of the dead bird. Dropping analysis will reveal most but not all 'carrier' birds. The tests are more reliable when the birds are under the stress of breeding or in an overcrowded aviary.

Look for a 'trigger' for a Megabacteria (Avian Gastric Yeast) outbreak when unrelated birds suddenly 'go light'. Megabacteria (Avian Gastric Yeast) is not highly contagious from bird to bird but reflects an increased susceptibility to the disease. Most birds recover spontaneously from Megabacteria (Avian Gastric Yeast) after the underlying disease process has been treated. Infection is also likely to recur after treatment when underlying diseases are left unattended. Look to concurrent diseases, overcrowding and weak individual families when recurrent Megabacteria (Avian Gastric Yeast) infections are experienced.

Treatment

Megabacteria (Avian Gastric Yeast) is cured by selecting genetically resistant birds for breeding, and controlling the diseases that may have weakened the immune system, notably Moulding Disease (Aflatoxicosis) and Ornithosis (*Chlamydophila*). It may infect birds during the juvenile moult when poor management conditions exist. Megabacteria (Avian Gastric Yeast) infection is also implicated with poor breeding results in many aviaries.

For years scientific research failed to find a medicine that actually killed this particularly large bacteria. Nowadays, the antifungal drug, amphotericin, is used to treat Megabacteria (Avian Gastric Yeast) infections in individual birds. Unfortunately, this medicine can cause kidney damage and infertility in healthy finches and its use should be restricted to infected and in-contact birds only.

Mite and Lice Infestations

Mite and lice infestations are an underestimated cause of decreased breeding performance and health in Gouldians. Red, biting and depluming mites are harmful to finches and cause intense irritation. They are light sensitive, fast moving and difficult to find. Birds stamping their feet and exhibiting signs of extreme agitation are often the best indicators that these mites are present.

Other species of mites and lice cause finches to jump suddenly, anxiously preen around the base of the tail, twitch and repeatedly stretch their legs. The unrest and weakness caused by these parasites often result in increased infertility (with birds too tired to breed), dead-in-shell (incubation failure) and illness in breeding hens.

In addition, blood-sucking mites and Air Sac Mite cause nestling, fledgling and adult deaths and are often the underlying cause of other diseases in finch aviaries. Always attempt to keep finches free of mites and lice.

Blood-sucking Mites

Red Mites *Dermanyssus* sp. bite the skin and suck the blood of nestlings and their parents, causing intense irritation and anaemia. They hide in crevices and cracks of the aviary and nests during the day and suck blood from the finches at night. At night they can be seen in the nest or aviary as very small red dots that move quickly away from the light of a torch. Treatment for Red Mite should occur during the day when the mites are in the crevices of the aviary. The Northern Mite *Ornithonyssus sylvarium*, another blood-sucking mite, spends its life entirely on the bird.

Blood-sucking mites cause respiratory symptoms, general depression, anaemia, and in heavy infestations can cause deaths of nestlings, fledglings and adult finches.

Epidermoptic Mites

These depluming mites cause a scaly skin irritation leading to wing, tail and back feather loss. It is considered to be one possible cause of baldness in Gouldians.

Air Sac Mites

Air Sac Mite *Sternostoma tracheacolum* is an internal parasite that lives in the airways and air sacs, causing irritation and respiratory infection. Heavy infestations cause breathing difficulties, wheezing, open-mouth breathing and death in fledglings and adult birds. Gouldians are very susceptible to Air Sac Mite infestations.

Heavy infestations may be seen with a light after wetting the neck of the birds. They appear as pinhead-sized spots moving up and down the trachea (windpipe). The Bengalese Finch is not as susceptible to Air Sac Mite infestation and is often used as foster-parents to help control infestation of this mite in Gouldian Finches.

Symptoms

- Squeaking.
- Coughing.
- Sneezing.
- Nasal discharge.
- Loss of voice.
- Head shaking.
- Gasping.

Treatment

Flock Treatment

Ivermectin should be administered to the entire flock for two consecutive days. The nests and aviary must be cleaned and disinfected with a pyrethrin (Coopex™) spray and then wiped over on the second day of treatment. This treatment must be repeated each week for three weeks to break the life cycle of the mite. Reinfestation is then prevented by treating the flock every three weeks during the hot months and each month during winter.

Individual Bird Treatment

Individual birds should be removed to the hospital cage for treatment. One drop of ivermectin should be applied to the skin of the neck each day for five days. Ivermectin should also be administered to the drinking water for three consecutive days.

Ornithosis (*Chlamydophila*) Infection

Gouldian Finch mutations are more vulnerable to the effects of Ornithosis, caused by infection from *Chlamydophila* organisms because of their inherent weakness. They are highly susceptible during the juvenile moult. Outside the breeding season some mutations infected with Ornithosis (*Chlamydophila*) may appear quite normal and come into breeding condition naturally. It is only after the start of breeding activity that they show signs of active Ornithosis (*Chlamydophila*) infection. These 'carrier' birds remain healthy in a protected and artificial environment such as box-type aviaries and indoor cages, but succumb to the effects of an active Ornithosis (*Chlamydophila*) infection when they are stressed. Cocks that 'carry' the disease fluff up and fall out of breeding condition while courting the hen, because a fragile immune system fails in response to the suppressive effect of testosterone. Hens that are 'carriers' break down and become ill during the energy-demanding process of laying eggs. Ornithosis (*Chlamydophila*) is the most common cause of infertility associated with dead-in-shell, dying babies and failure to go to nest and must be considered the most likely cause of infertility and poor breeding results in mutations housed in box-type aviaries or indoor cages.

Young finches in overcrowded outdoor aviaries may also become susceptible to Ornithosis (*Chlamydophila*) and should benefit from a short course of doxycycline. These birds must be removed from the aviary and treated in isolation.

Under good aviary conditions, finches housed in outdoor aviaries are naturally resistant to Ornithosis (*Chlamydophila*). However under poor conditions, this serious disease may appear and spread to adjacent aviaries because it is an airborne infection.

Symptoms

- Lethargy.
- Fluffing of the feathers.
- Half-closed (tired) eyelids.
- Watery eyes or a wet shoulder patch from rubbing at the eye.
- One-eye cold.
- Conjunctivitis.
- Beak stretching and scratching.
- Sneezing.
- Grey-green staining of the vent feathers.
- Failure to go to nest.

Ornithosis (*Chlamydophila*) should be considered a possible cause of occasional sudden death of finches or the intermittent but continuing death of finches of any age. Other conditions such as food contamination, overcrowding and nutritional deficiencies may also manifest in this way. Ornithosis should also be considered the most likely cause of breeding failure in an aviary that in the past has had good breeding results.

Treatment

The birds should be treated with doxycycline hydrochloride for between 21–30 days, the length of time determined by monitoring the response of the birds to treatment. Prolonged inappropriate treatment with doxycycline may also harm the immune system and cause infertility.

Metal (but not stainless steel) containers and minerals present in shell grits, sand, deep litter and mineral supplements have a negating effect on the proper absorption of tetracyclines (including doxycycline) into the bird's body. In the past it has been necessary to remove all minerals and metal containers in order to achieve a full therapeutic effect from doxycycline. However, removal of minerals during doxycycline treatments has been found to inhibit recovery, especially for breeding finches. Minerals may now be fed when citric acid is added to the drinking water during doxycycline treatment.

Treatment using doxycycline is of great benefit to mutations and weak families of finches kept in cages or box-type aviaries, because Ornithosis may harm their immune system irreversibly and render them susceptible to future illness. Polyomavirus, Streptococcal and Thrush (*Candida*) infections disappear when Ornithosis is controlled.

A doxycycline treatment should be administered to all weak mutation families prior to breeding to help them eliminate Ornithosis and prepare for breeding. Careful observation during the breeding cycle is then necessary to identify weak individuals. These birds and pairs may need treatment during breeding if fertile eggs are to be produced. Doxycycline must not be administered after a strong mutation family has become established from the original weak bloodlines because further treatment may produce infertility and an unsustainable family of mutations.

For Gouldian mutations, a trial doxycycline treatment prior to the breeding season may be used to identify the Ornithosis status of each individual bird. Individual birds showing a positive response to doxycyline treatment are likely to be 'carriers' and should benefit from further treatment prior to or during breeding. Previously strong individuals that respond negatively to the doxycycline treatment are unlikely 'carriers' and will not benefit from doxycycline. These are strong individuals that should be paired and housed together in a box-type aviary or indoor cages. The strong birds must not receive doxycycline and should become foundation pairs that help establish the desired mutation.

Doxycycline should be given to mutation juveniles soon after they are removed from their parents and placed into the young bird flight. A short treatment often invigorates young mutations, protects their naturally developing resistance and helps create and establish a stronger family.

Polyomavirus

Polyomavirus, a disease that may permanently damage the immune system, is a disease of the breeding season that affects nestlings. Adult birds cannot become infected. Infected birds become incapable of repelling germs that do not affect Normal Gouldian Finches. The result is sickly individuals that are the first to fall ill when conditions are less than perfect. Infected young become 'carriers' for life. The immune system of carrier birds is permanently damaged by Polyomavirus.

Nestlings from a clutch of mutations and split mutations are always the first to become ill in the nest or after they fledge. This fact further supports a susceptibility of mutations to the effects of Polyomavirus. A susceptibility to Coccidiosis, Ornithosis (*Chlamydophila*), Thrush (*Candida*), *Cochlosoma*, *Campylobacter* and Streptococcal infections may be the result of underlying Polyomavirus infection (or vice versa).

Polyomavirus, Ornithosis (*Chlamydophila*) and Thrush (*Candida*) were often involved with deaths of Yellow mutations as they were being established in Australia (Marshall 1990). Improving nutrition, hygiene and the preparation of softfoods controlled Thrush (*Candida*). Polyomavirus infections were lessened after the Ornithosis (*Chlamydophila*) was managed. Selective breeding finally eliminated it. Yellow Gouldians are now considered a strong mutation.

Weakness in Blue mutation Gouldians may similarly be the result of underlying Polyomavirus and Ornithosis (*Chlamydophila*) infections. The prevalence of Streptococcal infection—rather than Thrush (*Candida*)—points towards Polyomavirus as the primary cause of weakness in Blue mutation families. This weakness is then perpetuated as Polyomavirus is passed onto offspring.

L & J MCGINNIS

Malocclusion of the beak may be associated with mineral deficiencies, congenital abnormalities and Polyomavirus infection. Gouldians with cross beaks may exist happily but are not recommended as breeding stock.

Polyomavirus must be controlled in order to establish strong Blue mutation families. This may be achieved by first treating for Ornithosis (*Chlamydophila*) and maintaining good housing, care, hygiene and feeding. Proven healthy and successful Normal Gouldians must then be crossbred with Blue mutations. The most robust splits from these pairings should form the basis of a new Blue mutation family. The chances of producing hardy Blues that are also free of Polyomavirus are improved by employing this health and breeding sequence.

Symptoms

Nestlings

- Sudden death of nestlings at any age.
- Retarded growth.
- Anaemia. (Nestlings become pale in colour and are weak.)
- Rejection of weaklings by parents.

Adults
- Pale, elongated beak.
- Failure to come into breeding condition.
- Lack of vitality.
- Non-specific illness related to changes in the weather (ie 'fluffed-up' appearance).
- Recurring infections.

Treatment

Treatment for Polyomavirus relies upon the elimination of carrier birds. Fanciers must identify those birds that are carriers and not include them in the breeding program. The elimination of any stress factors is integral to managing Polyomavirus carriers correctly. Underlying disease, poor nutrition and other stresses are major contributing factors to this disease. In order to control Polyomavirus naturally, it is important to eliminate all stress factors.

When an outbreak of Polyomavirus is experienced during breeding, all carrier birds should be identified and removed from the breeding program. Breeding may still continue from those pairs that are healthy.

Salmonella Infection

Salmonella infection is regarded as a serious disease of Gouldians housed in ornamental or half-open aviaries and is difficult to eradicate. Even the strongest medicines are unable to cure genetically weak families susceptible to *Salmonella* because recovered birds remain 'carriers' for life. These 'carriers' spread the disease to other birds and future generations. The only way to eradicate *Salmonella* in these birds is through primary prevention, which is achievable by a combination of two methods: firstly by using *Salmonella*-resistant families as breeders and secondly by ensuring that rodents (rats and mice) and vermin (cockroaches) are regularly controlled. Newly introduced breeder hens that produce dead-in-shell chicks within their first year of breeding are assumed to be 'carriers' and must be culled.

Gouldians housed in outdoor aviaries are usually naturally resistant to *Salmonella* and should be able to repel the effects of newly introduced 'carrier' birds, but may be unable to resist infections introduced by rodents. *Salmonella* infection is less of a problem for Gouldians housed in indoor cages and box-type aviaries where rodent control is strict. Gouldian mutations and weak inbred families of specialist finches are more susceptible to the introduction of *Salmonella*.

Symptoms

Salmonella causes a wide variety of symptoms and spreads slowly—weeks rather than days—through a flock of breeding birds.

Nestlings
- Pipping deaths.
- Red-coloured, dehydrated nestlings.
- Dead chicks aged 1–5 days.

Fledglings
- Watery eyes.
- Nasal discharge.
- Conjunctivitis.
- Smelly, pasted vents.
- Weight loss.
- Neurological signs.
- Lameness.
- Inability to fly.

Salmonella should be assumed as the cause of sudden illness or death in breeding hens when rodents are found in the aviary or food storage area.

Treatment

Enrofloxacin (Baytril™) is the first-choice treatment against *Salmonella* infection. It should be administered to the entire flock for 10 consecutive days. Mice, rats and cockroaches must be eradicated during the treatment to prevent reinfection. The aviary must also be disinfected and rodent droppings removed. *Salmonella* is preventable by the use of concealed rodent baits in the aviaries, especially in winter.

Streptococcal Infection

Inherently weak birds, eg Gouldian Finch mutations housed indoors, are most susceptible to Streptococcal (*Streptococcus faecalis*, also known as *Enterococcus faecalis*) infections, which are a common cause of eye problems, infertility and deaths in mutations. However, infection may also appear in overcrowded, unhygienic outdoor aviaries, where large amounts of *Streptococcus* germs are present. Young birds are particularly susceptible to infection. The nest may become wet and after a short time will emit a characteristic smell. In the early stages of infection there is no smell to the dropping. Finch enthusiasts should learn to differentiate the different smells of enteritis because *Streptococcus*, *E. coli*, *Salmonella* and yeast (*Candida*) infections each produce a distinctive smell.

Weaklings housed in spotlessly clean, indoor cages may also become infected with innocuous strains of *Streptococcus*. Breeding, young or mutation finches are more susceptible to the effects of a diet low in protein, carbohydrates, minerals or vitamins, cold stress, mite infestations, dusty, unclean aviaries or overcrowding and are therefore the most likely to succumb to the disease.

Streptococcal infections are associated with diseases that weaken the immune system. For example, birds 'carrying' Polyomavirus, Ornithosis (*Chlamydophila*), tapeworms or gizzardworms become susceptible to *Streptococcus* infection. Weak families of Gouldian mutations, especially juveniles, are the most likely candidates for Polyomavirus-induced Streptococcal infections.

Introduced breeding pairs are the most common cause of *Streptococcus* infection in aviaries with previously good breeding results. New birds should be monitored for stress and fatigue. These are early signs of *Streptococcus* infection that may be alleviated by offering energy supplements to breeding birds.

Breeding birds can also be protected from *Streptococcus* infection by eradicating mites and lice that cause irritation and restlessness. Dust control helps clean the environment enjoyed by *Streptococcus* germs. Regular vitamin A supplementation improves the health of birds' sinuses, protecting them from *Streptococcus*-induced sinus infections.

Streptococcus infections may suddenly appear or persist in a more chronic form. *Streptococcus* infections that occur suddenly are always related to stress and may infect previously healthy robust individuals. There is a high mortality rate, with many breeding birds dying suddenly. The chronic form appears more frequently in mutation finches housed indoors and birds weakened by 'carrier' type diseases.

Symptoms

Streptococcus infection should be considered the cause of the following symptoms until proven otherwise:

- The sudden appearance of sickness in a cock during or shortly after courtship activity.
- Uterine infection in breeding hens.
- Sudden death on the nest.
- Dead-in-shell chicks. Birds that hatch may grow slowly and often die.
- Skin irritations and foot infections.
- The appearance of respiratory symptoms in breeding birds at any part of the breeding cycle, eg tail bobbing, laboured breathing, noisy, clicking respiration, coughing, sneezing and beak scratching.

- The appearance of enteritis symptoms in breeding birds at any part of the breeding cycle, eg diarrhoea, dirty, wet or pasted vent feathers, dirty stained tails or large, brown watery droppings that carry no odour.

Symptoms of *Streptococcus* infections closely resemble those seen when serious outbreaks of Ornithosis (*Chlamydophila*) occur. Some symptoms of *Streptococcus* infections also resemble Air Sac Mite infection and *Mycoplasma*.

Treatment

Antibiotics in the form of a penicillin-type drug should be administered in the drinking water of sick individuals that have been removed from the flock into a warmed hospital cage for treatment.

Antibiotics should not be administered to the entire flock unless *Streptococcus* infection has been confirmed by veterinary analysis and then only when birds are dying. However, if the birds are sick but not dying, the aviary should be cleaned and a strong water cleanser added to the drinking water of the aviary.

Thrush (Candidiasis)

Thrush (*Candida*) is caused by a yeast *Candida albicans* and is common in Gouldian Finches. The organism invades the lining of the upper digestive tract (mouth, oesophagus, crop and proventiculus) and the koilin lining of the ventriculus (gizzard). Thrush damages this lining, prevents the gizzard from grinding seed and is a common cause of undigested seed in the droppings. (*Cochlosoma* infections and Megabacteria (Avian Gastric Yeast) infection are other causes of undigested seed found in the droppings.)

Infection appears when the birds are under stress. Stressful conditions that possibly predispose finches to Thrush include an unbalanced diet (especially vitamin A deficiency); poor hygiene; crowded conditions; excessive moisture and food spoilage; poor aviary design; and the uncontrolled use of antibiotics. A weak genetic lineage may also predispose finches to Thrush infection.

A microscopic (400X) view of yeast Candida spp. organisms. This organism is a simple oval shape. It reproduces by splitting into two organisms. Just prior to splitting, the yeast resembles a figure of eight (referred to as a budding form). Red arrow: budding yeast organism. Blue arrow: a cluster of single yeast organisms.

Thrush in nestlings and recent fledglings cause crop stasis. The failure of the crop to empty quickly promotes fermentation visible as air in the crop. Nestlings with Thrush infections grow poorly, become red with dehydration and may vomit. They often die with a 'doughy', thick-walled and air-filled 'bloating' crop.

The presence of Thrush in droppings of Gouldians reflects an immune system under attack and not coping well. Anything that suppresses the immune system may predispose Gouldians to Thrush (*Candida*) infection. Often other diseases damage the immune system, allowing Thrush (*Candida*) to invade the bowel. For example, Thrush (*Candida*) often accompanies *E. coli* and fungal infections, Ornithosis (*Chlamydophila*), Polyomavirus, Coccidiosis and worm infestations.

Symptoms

- Thrush (*Candida*) infections produce ulcerations of the mouth, crop, stomach and bowel. These painful sores produce a 'stomach-ache' stance, the head of the infected bird hunching over the crop.

- Infected birds eat less, lose energy, become listless and exhibit a typical fluffed-up appearance of a sick finch.
- Severely infected finches are disinterested in their surroundings, appear tired, may vomit, swallow excessively, sneeze after drinking, become dull and dry in the feather (a sign of dehydration) and rapidly lose body condition.
- At first the droppings are wet but then turn dark forest-green in colour, are sticky and often contain whole or partially digested seed. White urates may also stain the vent and tail.

Treatment

Thrush (*Candida*) medication will give only temporary relief and will not be totally effective until the underlying disease(s) have been treated.

Nystatin™ is the first choice medicine for treating sick individuals in the hospital cage when the cause of the illness is Thrush (*Candida*).

Cochlosoma

Gouldian Finches are highly susceptible to *Cochlosoma* infection because they have no evolutionary immunity to the disease. Birds that have recovered may remain infected for life. *Cochlosoma*—flagellated protozoan parasites that inhabit the gastrointestinal tract of finches—are a common disease-causing agent in mixed collections that include Gouldian Finches and should be assumed to be the cause of nestling deaths of other Australian finch species when they are housed together with Gouldians. The infection also affects Gouldians housed as a single-species colony and Gouldians housed indoors that rear their own young or use Bengalese Finches as foster-parents. It is a cause of high mortality in nestling and juvenile Gouldians, especially those reared by Bengalese foster-parents that are carriers of this disease.

Note: the selection of *Cochlosoma*-free families of Bengalese to control the infection in Gouldians is difficult to achieve, because Bengalese may appear extremely healthy, but may in fact be 'carriers' of *Cochlosoma* infection. It is difficult to eliminate the disease from the species. They may also carry *Campylobacter* and Polyomavirus infections. *Cochlosoma* should be suspected as the cause of whole or partially digested seed in droppings of Gouldians reared by Bengalese Finch foster-parents. The foster-parents exhibit watery droppings but show no other sign of illness.

Symptoms

Finches of any age may show symptoms.

Nestlings at Pin-feather Age (8–10 Days of Age)
- Stunted growth.
- Red and shrivelled appearance.
- High numbers of deaths.
- Whole or partially digested seed in the droppings.

Fledglings
- Fluffed-up appearance and weakness.
- Evidence of 'going light'.
- Difficulties with moult, eg slow or stuck-in-the-moult.
- Yellow staining of droppings on tail or vent feathers.
- Whole or partially digested seed in the droppings.

Adults and Parents
- Fluffed-up appearance and lifelessness.
- Lack of breeding condition is evidenced by pallor of plumage colour, no shine to plumage, beak colour of hens turns pale and birds stop singing.
- Wet, stained vent.
- Weight loss.
- Dull eyes.

Treatment

Ronidazole, administered for two or three days every week, is the best way to control *Cochlosoma*. It also promotes immunity against reinfection and appears to be the best way to improve breeding results, especially when establishing weak mutations. Ronidazole treatment should not be used after a mutation has been established. An initial treatment program using ronidasole must be given to outdoor aviaries and mixed collections in order to save nestlings. However, identifying and culling weak families and replacing Bengalese with strong Gouldian foster-parents where possible remain the only long-term answer to *Cochlosoma* infection. The administration of a strong water cleanser in the drinking water for two days each week, will also control *Cochlosoma* infection in Gouldians.

The administration of ronidasole in the drinking water of affected birds will produce a very rapid positive response within 48 hours. Parent birds brighten up almost immediately within 24 hours. Wet nests dry up, nestlings start to thrive and mortality ceases within 48–72 hours.

Recovered birds remain as 'carriers' and a source of recurrent infection, especially in mixed collections housed in outdoor aviaries, where it is difficult to identify the 'carriers' and therefore control *Cochlosoma* infections. Ronidazole should be administered during the breeding season and the juvenile moult to the entire flock when *Cochlosoma* is a problem. Repeat and ongoing treatment at these times helps nestlings and juveniles develop their own natural resistance against the disease. As adults they should then be totally resistant to further infection.

Worms

Worms rob infested birds of nutrients, weaken them and may cause death from obstruction of the bowel.

Roundworms are very rare in finches. However, hairworms are more common in outdoor aviaries with earth floors. These floors may harbour infective eggs for many years. It is difficult to know the prevalence of gizzardworms and cropworms unless partially digested or whole seeds are seen in the droppings.

Gouldians housed in outdoor aviaries should receive regular tapeworm and gizzardworm treatments—if they are housed in an environment, particularly a mixed collection, where birds are fed livefood or insects. Although generally Gouldian Finches do not consume livefood or insects, if ingested, they may become infested by tapeworm or gizzardworm. These worms are rarely encountered in Gouldians housed indoors (in cages or box-type aviaries).

Roundworms, hairworms, tapeworms and gizzardworms may be diagnosed by the microscopic examination of droppings.

Regular worming of Gouldians controls most worm problems with minimum effort, but it is important to know how and when the best worm treatment should be used. Some worm treatments cannot be given during the moult and others cannot be given during breeding.

Tapeworm (Cestodes)

Gouldian Finches do not require the addition of livefood (Marshall and Lewis pers. comm.) Therefore tapeworms are an uncommon occurrence in Gouldian Finches. If infested with tapeworms the bowel is prevented from absorbing the nutrients into the body, resulting in weight loss, poor feather quality, possible anaemia, lethargy during breeding and susceptibility to illness. Breeding finches infested with worms become susceptible to enteritis, bacterial, yeast and fungal diseases. As a result, they are unable to rear babies successfully. Parents infested with tapeworm often reject their young.

Tapeworms are very difficult to detect unless the worms are seen hanging from the vent. Tapeworms become a serious problem when large numbers obstruct the intestine and cause 'going light', diarrhoea and death. Tapeworm problems worsen as the number of insects eaten increases. Heavily planted aviaries with compost heaps present the most risk from tapeworm-related deaths. They do not spread from bird to bird and need a third host, with ants, cockroaches, slugs, moths, weevils and other insects acting as hosts to spread the infection.

Treatment

Total eradication of tapeworms in finch aviaries requires the simultaneous eradication of those insects that spread the disease. Pyrethrin sprays, ie Coopex™, are commonly used and safe for finches.

Total eradication of tapeworms is only possible when finches are housed in insect-proof cages and livefood is not provided. A wormer that contains praziquantel must be administered to the flock for two consecutive days each month throughout the entire year. This treatment does not impair the natural health of the flock.

Yersinia Infection

Yersinia is a common cause of sudden death in finches housed in outdoor aviaries where rodent control is poor. Most *Yersinia* infections are seen in winter and associated with mice. Infected birds suffer diarrhoea and 'go light' very quickly. Mortality is high, with birds dying suddenly. Infection is uncommon in Gouldians housed in rodent-proofed, indoor or box-type aviaries. Affected birds are often too sick to respond to therapy but eradication of rodents and administering Baytril™ to the entire flock should stop deaths within one week. *Yersinia* is diagnosed during a post-mortem by pin-point (sometimes large), pale-coloured abscesses that cover the liver and spleen.

BIBLIOGRAPHY

Australian Birdkeeper 1991, *A Guide to Gouldian Finches, Their Care and Management*, ABK Publications, New South Wales.

Brush, AH & Seifried, H 1968, 'Pigmentation and Feather Structure in Genetic Variants of Gouldian Finch, *Peophila gouldiae*', *Auk*, vol. 85, The American Ornithologists Union, USA, pp. 416–430.

Burton, CT & Weathers, WW 2003, 'Energetics and Thermoregulation of the Gouldian Finch (*Erythrura gouldiae*)', *Emu*, vol. 103(1), pp. 1–10.

Christidis, L & Boles, WE 1994, 'The Taxonomy and Species of Birds of Australia and its Territories', *Royal Australasian Ornithologists Union Monograph*, No. 2, RAOU, Melbourne.

Christidis, L & Schodde, R 1991, 'Relationships of Australo-Papuan Songbirds—Protein Evidence', *Ibis*, vol. 133, pp. 277–285.

Clement, P, Harris, A & Davis, J 1993, *Finches and Sparrows, An Identification Guide*, Christopher Helm Ltd, London, p. 500.

Delacour, J 1943, 'A Revision of the Subfamily Estrildinae of the Family Ploceidae', *Zoologica*, vol. 28, New York Society, pp. 69–86.

Dostine, P 1998, *Gouldian Finch Recovery Plan*, Environment Australia, Canberra.

Dostine, PL & Franklin, DC 2002, 'A Comparison of the Diet of Three Finch Species in the Yinberrie Hills Area, Northern Territory', *Emu*, vol. 102, pp. 159–164.

Dostine, PL, Johnson, GC, Franklin, DC, Zhang, Y & Hempel, C 2001, 'Seasonal Use of Savanna Landscapes by the Gouldian Finch, *Erythrura gouldiae*, in the Yinberrie Hills Area, Northern Territory', *Australian Wildlife Research*, vol. 28(4), pp. 445–458.

Feduccia, A 1996, *The Origin and Evolution of Birds*, Yale University Press, New Haven, p. 346.

Forrester, RI & Wood, JT 1999, 'Estimating the Abundance of the Gouldian, Long-tailed and Masked Finches in the Yinberrie Hills', *CSIRO Report*, pp. 1–14.

Fox, S, Brooks, R, Lewis, MJ & Johnson, CN 2002, 'Polymorphism, Mate Choice and Sexual Selection in the Gouldian Finch (*Erythrura gouldiae*)', *Australian Journal of Zoology*, vol. 50(2), pp. 125–134.

Franklin, DC, Burbidge, AH & Dostine, PL 1999, 'The Harvest of Wild Birds for Aviculture: An Historical Perspective on Finch Trapping in the Kimberley with Special Emphasis on the Gouldian Finch', *Australian Zoologist*, vol. 31, pp. 92–109.

Garnett, ST & Crowley, GM 2000, *The Action Plan for Australian Birds 2000*, Environment Australia, Canberra.

Goodwin, D 1982, *Estrildid Finches of the World*, British Museum of Natural History, Oxford University Press, Oxford.

Gould, J 1865, *Handbook of the Birds of Australia*, Gould, London.

Hall, FM 1962, *The Symposium for the Zoological Society of London*, UK.

Immelmann, K 1977, *Australian Finches in Bush and Aviary*, Angus and Robertson, London.

King, AS & Mclelland, J 1984, *Birds: Their Structure and Function*, 2nd edn, Bailliere Tindall, London, pp. 104–105.

Kingston, RJ 1994, *A Complete Manual for the Keeping and Breeding of Finches*, Indruss Productions, p. 480.

Leaney, J & Williams, F 1993, *The Australian Canary Handbook*, Impact Printing, Melbourne, p. 246.

Lewis, MJ (in review), 'Seeding patterns of the native Australian savanna grasses *Alloteropsis semialata*, *Chrysopogon fallax* and *Triodia bitextura* in relation to fire intensity and their influence in determining population fluctuations in the endangered Gouldian Finch *Erythrura gouldiae*'.

Lewis, MJ 2003, 'Saving the Endangered Gouldian Finch: Landscape Fire Management for Healthier Savanna Grasslands', *Third International Wildlife Management Congress*, Christchurch.

Lewis, MJ, Lewis, J & Lewis, J 2000, *A Guide to Zebra Finches*, ABK Publications, New South Wales.

Marshall, R 1990, *AAV Conference Proceedings*, Australia.

Marshall, R 2003, *Gouldian and Finch Health*, Carlingford Animal Hospital, New South Wales.

Massa, R, Stradi, R 1999, *Colori in volo: il piumaggio degli uccelli ricerca scientifica e cultura umanistica*, Università degli Studi di Milano & Hoepli, Milan.

McGraw, KJ, Hill, GE & Parker, RS 2003, 'Carotenoid Pigments in a Mutant Cardinal: Implications for the Genetic and Enzymatic Control Mechanisms of Carotenoid Metabolism in Birds', *The Condor*, vol. 105, The Cooper Ornithological Society, USA, pp. 587–592.

Mitchell, MA & Tully, TN (eds) 2003, *Seminars in Avian and Exotic Pet Medicine*, vol. 12(1), pp. 12–22.

Morris, D 1958, 'The Comparative Ethology of Grassfinches (*Erythrurae*) and Mannikins (*Amadinae*)', *Proceedings of the Zoological Society of London*, vol. 131, pp. 389–439.

Petrak, ML (ed.) 1982, *Diseases of Cage and Aviary Birds*, 2nd edn, Lea & Febiger, Philadelphia, p. 189.

Pizzey, G 1980, *The Field Guide to the Birds of Australia*, Collins, Sydney.

Pizzey, G 2003, *The Field Guide to the Birds of Australia*, HarperCollins Publishers, Sydney, p. 496.

Proctor, N & Lynch, P 1993, *Manual of Ornithology: Avian Structure and Function*, Yale University Press, New Haven, p. 18.

Prum, RO, Torres, R, Williamson, S & Dyck, J 1999, 'Two-dimensional Fourier Analysis of the Spongy Medullary Keratin of Structurally Coloured Feather Barbs', *Proceedings of the Royal Society Biological Sciences Series* 266 (1414), London, pp. 13–22.

Ritchie, B, Harrison, G & Harrison, L 1994, *Avian Medicine: Principles and Application*, Wingers Publishing Inc, Florida, p. 1187.

Slater, P, Slater, P & Slater, R 1986, *The Slater Field Guide to Australian Birds*, Lansdowne Publishing, Australia.

Strahan, R 1996, 'Finches, Bowerbirds and Other Passerines of Australia', *National Photographic Index of Australian Wildlife*, Angus and Robertson, Australia, p. 301.

Taylor, D 2002, 'Breeding Matters', *Cage and Aviary Birds*, February (2), p. 3.

Tidemann, SC 1986, 'Relationships Between Finches and Pastoral Practices in Northern Australia', *Proceedings of General Meetings of the Working Group on Granivorous Birds*, INTECOL, Ottawa, Canada, June 28, pp. 304–314.

Tidemann, SC 1987, 'Gouldian Finches in the Wild', *Bird Keeping in Australia*, vol. 30(10), pp. 145–153.

Tidemann, SC & Boydon, J 1992a, 'Comparison of the Breeding Sites and Habitat of Two Hole-nesting Estrildid Finches, One Endangered, in Northern Australia', *Journal of Tropical Ecology*, vol. 8, pp. 373–388.

Tidemann, SC & Lawson, C 1999, 'Breeding Biology of the Gouldian Finch *Erythrura gouldiae* an Endangered Finch of Northern Australia', *Emu*, vol. 99, pp. 191–199.

Tidemann, SC & McOrist, S 1992b, 'Parasitism of Wild Gouldian Finches (*Erythrura gouldiae*) by the Air-sac Mite *Sternostoma tracheacolum*', *Wildlife Diseases*, vol. 28(1), pp. 80–84.

Tidemann, SC & Woinarski, JCZ 1994, 'Moult Characteristics and Breeding Seasons of Gouldian *Erythrura gouldiae*, Masked *Poephila personata* and Long-tailed Finches *P. acuticauda* in Savannah Woodland in the Northern Territory', *Emu*, vol. 94, pp. 46–52.

Van den Abeele, D 2003, 'Gouldians Go Head to Head', *Cage and Aviary Birds*, September, pp. 10–11.

Volker, O 1964, 'Die gelben Mutanten des Rotbauchwurgers (*Laniarius atrococcineus*) und der Gouldamandine (*Chloebia gouldiae*) in biochemischer Sicht', *J. Ornithol.*, vol. 30, pp. 97–117.

Woinarski, JCZ 1990, 'Effects of Fire on the Bird Communities of Tropical Woodlands and Open Forests in Northern Australia', *Australian Journal of Ecology*, vol. 15, pp. 1–22.

Woinarski, JCZ & Tidemann, S 1992, 'Survivorship and Some Population Parameters for the Endangered Gouldian Finch *Erythrura gouldiae* and Two Other Finch Species at Two Sites in Tropical Northern Australia', *Emu*, vol. 92, pp. 33–38.

Zann, R 1996, *The Zebra Finch, A Synthesis of Field and Laboratory Studies*, Oxford University Press, Oxford.

Ziegler, G 1975, *The Gouldian Finch*, trans by Australian Finch Society, Bristol.

Ziswiler, V, Guttinger, RH & Bregulla, H 1972, 'Monographie der Gattung *Erythrura* Swainson 1873 (Aves, Passeres, Estrilididae)', *Bonner Zoologische Monographien*, No. 2, Bonn.

The Acclaimed 'A Guide to...' series.

A Guide to Australian Grassfinches

The popularity of Australian Grassfinches worldwide is largely due to the hardiness of these tiny, gregarious and colourful birds. The 18 members of the Grassfinch family Estrildae recognised in Australia are featured in detail. Diagrams indicating visual differences and some 160 colour photographs support the 80 pages of text. A must for every finch breeder's library.

Author: Russell Kingston
ISBN 0 9587102 28   80 Pages

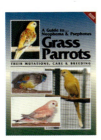

A Guide to Neophema and Psephotus Grass Parrots and Their Mutations (Revised Edition)

This title features over 160 full colour images of mutations in the Neophema and Psephotus grass parrot group. Details include breeding expectations, housing, feeding and general management.

Author: Toby Martin
ISBN 0 9587102 44   88 Pages

A Guide to Asiatic Parrots and Their Mutations (Revised Edition)

Containing over 70 colour images of Asiatic parrot mutations, this title also features genetic tables and information on nutrition, housing and breeding.

Authors: Syd & Jack Smith
ISBN 0 9587102 52   88 Pages

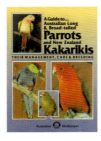

A Guide to Australian Long and Broad-tailed Parrots and New Zealand Kakarikis

This full colour title features beautiful photography throughout. Each of the 12 species is featured in its own chapter with distribution maps and general information specific to that species including management, diet and nutrition, housing requirements, breeding, handrearing, sexing and mutations.

Author: Kevin Wilson
ISBN 0 9587455 36   88 Pages

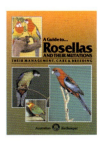

A Guide to Rosellas and Their Mutations

This full colour title features the general management, care and breeding of the Platycercus genus. Breeding expectations, including genetic tables and mutations, are discussed for each species and their subspecies. Beautiful photography throughout.

Author: Australian Birdkeeper
ISBN 0 9587455 52   80 Pages

A Guide to Cockatiels and Their Mutations

Written by two of Australia's foremost Cockatiel breeders, this 96-page title features beautiful colour photography, including all known mutations. Excellent easy-to-read information covers the care, management, housing and breeding of these popular birds.

Authors: Peggy Cross and Diana Andersen
ISBN 0 9587455 87   96 Pages

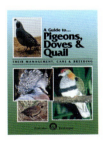

A Guide to Pigeons, Doves and Quail

A world first in aviculture, this title covers all species in this group available to the Australian aviculturist. Stunning colour photography throughout is supported by precise, easy-to-read information on the care, management, health and breeding of these unique birds.

Author: Danny Brown   184 Pages
ISBN 0 6462305 81

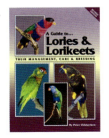

A Guide to Lories and Lorikeets (Revised Edition)

Completely reformatted and revised, including new sections on Lories and Lorikeets as Pets, Diseases and Disorders, Colour Mutations and Breeding Expectations, Peter Odekerken's A Guide to Lories and Lorikeets is bigger, better and more colourful than the highly successful original edition. Peter's exceptional photography again is beautifully supportive of the informative text which together make this a must-have title.

Author: Peter Odekerken
ISBN 0 9587445 95   152 Pages

A Guide to Basic Health and Disease in Birds (Revised Edition)

Since its first publication in 1996, A Guide to Basic Health & Disease in Birds has proven to be one of the most sought after and respected titles worldwide in this generic range of avian publications. It is a credit to the author, Dr Michael Cannon. His devotion and concern for all aspects of avian health and husbandry have again been reflected in this revised edition.

Author: Dr Michael Cannon
ISBN 0 6462305 73   112 Pages

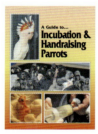

A Guide to Incubation & Handraising Parrots

This 104-page full colour title covers all necessary requirements needed to successfully take an egg through to a fully weaned chick. Beautifully illustrated with colour images throughout, this valuable title also includes many charts and diagrams and informative text laid out in an easy-to-read format. An invaluable reference for any serious bird breeder.

Author: Phil Digney
ISBN 0 9587102 1 X   104 Pages

A Guide to Pet & Companion Birds

This informative and often amusing 'introduction to bird keeping' appeals not only to the novice or want-to-be bird keeper, but also to the seasoned aviculturist looking for a refresher on the basics. This 96-page full colour book also guides you through the growing pains of increasing your bird family, including what to do when your birds have gone forth and multiplied.

Authors: Ray Dorge and Gail Sibley
ISBN 0 9587266 12   96 Pages

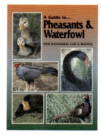

A Guide to Pheasants & Waterfowl

Dr Danny Brown the author of the highly regarded A Guide to Pigeons, Doves & Quail, has produced this superlative title on pheasants and waterfowl. The informative, easy-to-read text is lavishly supported with beautiful colour images throughout. Covering all aspects of care, housing, management and breeding of these unique birds, this title is a credit to the author and an ideal reference source.

Author: Dr Danny Brown
ISBN 0 9587102 36   248 Pages

A Guide to Australian White Cockatoos

Richly illustrated and full of practical hints, this well-researched, well-written book features facets of the author's personal experience with the Australian White Cockatoo family which shine throughout its 112 full colour pages on general management, care and breeding.

Author: Chris Hunt
ISBN: 0 9577024 1 8   112 Pages

A Guide to Zebra Finches

This title features 96 pages of easy-to-read, highly informative text, including all currently recognised Australian colour varieties of these internationally popular endemic birds. Full colour throughout, this book is a must for any Zebra Finch enthusiast.

Authors: Milton, John and Joan Lewis
ISBN 0 9577024 2 6   96 Pages

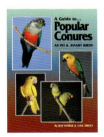

A Guide to Popular Conures

Featuring 13 of the most popular conures kept as pet or aviary birds throughout the world, this title is packed with easy-to-read, highly usable information and features superb full colour photographs throughout. Combined with their own experiences, Ray Dorge and Gail Sibley have recorded the results of an extensive research of large conure breeders. This title is sure to satisfy all fanciers and breeders of these wonderful parrots.

Authors: Ray Dorge & Gail Sibley
ISBN 0 9577024 3 4   112 Pages

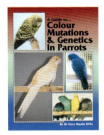

A Guide to Colour Mutations and Genetics in Parrots

This title, that has taken Australian author, Dr Terry Martin BVSc, some five years to complete, is the most definitive, collective work ever attempted on this intriguing and contentious subject. Drawing on information from specialist parrot mutation breeders from all over the world, Terry Martin has collated over 700 colour photographs in this 296-page soft and hard cover title within text that is both approachable and easily understood.

Author: Dr Terry Martin
ISBN: 0 9577024 69 (Soft cover)
ISBN: 0 9577024 77 (Hard cover)   296 Pages

A Guide to Macaws as Pet and Aviary Birds

Recognised internationally as one of the world's most accomplished and talented aviculturists, published author and speaker, Rick Jordan has produced the perfect companion book for anybody interested in macaws, be it as a pet or as breeding birds. Featuring spectacular full colour photography throughout, this 136-page soft cover title is packed with valuable and highly useable information.

Author: Rick Jordan
ISBN: 0 9577024 9 3   136 Pages

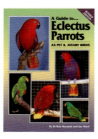

A Guide to Eclectus Parrots as Pet and Aviary Birds

This revised edition features a comprehensive description of all 10 subspecies, their taxonomy and identification. Other chapters include Eclectus in the Wild, Eclectus in Captivity—As Pet and Aviary Birds, Housing, Feeding, Breeding, Artificial Incubation and Handraising, Troubleshooting and Symptoms of Breeding Failure, Taming and Training, Colour Mutations and Genetics, Diseases and Disorders. Featuring over 250 colour photographs, this 160-page title is available in both soft and hard cover format.

Authors: Dr Rob Marshall & Ian Ward
ISBN: 0 9750817 0 5 (Soft cover)
ISBN: 0 9750817 0 5 (Hard cover)   160 Pages

Under the Microscope—Microscope Use and Pathogen Identification in Birds and Reptiles

This 56-page full colour, easy-to-read reference on microscope use and pathogen identification in birds and reptiles is a must for aviculturists and herpetologists with a desire to be in control of health problems in their collections.

Author: Dr Danny Brown
ISBN: 0 9577024 8 5   56 Pages

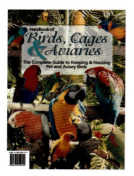

Handbook of Birds, Cages and Aviaries

This handbook provides a complete overview to the selection, keeping, management and care of both pet and aviary birds from individual pets to larger aviary complexes. Topics include Choosing your Bird, Housing and Keeping Pet Birds, Housing and Keeping Aviary Birds, Aviary Design, Construction and Management, Plantscaping your Aviary, Nutrition and Feeding, Breeding and Husbandry, General Management and Health and Disease Aspects. A must for the novice and serious aviculturist and all pet bird owners.

Edited by: ABK Publications
ISBN 0 9587102 95   128 Pages

Simply the best publications on pet & aviary birds available ...

AUSTRALIAN BirdKeeper MAGAZINE

Six glossy, colourful and informative issues per year.
Featuring articles written by top breeders and avian veterinarians from all over the world.

SUBSCRIPTIONS AVAILABLE

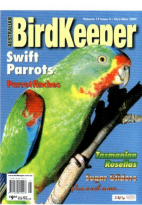

For further information or free catalogue contact

PUBLICATIONS
P.O. Box 6288
South Tweed Heads
NSW 2486 Australia
Phone: (07) 5590 7777 Fax: (07) 5590 7130
Email: birdkeeper@birdkeeper.com.au
Website: www.birdkeeper.com.au

NOTES

NOTES

NOTES